"Discover your inner superpowers and become a real-life superhero with this empowering, step-by-step guide. Learn h[...]te your armor of super skills, and unveil you[...] [...]u are worth it. You are a superhero."

—Janina Scarlet, PhD, award-winn[...]

"In *Be Mighty*, Stoddard offers a bold and compassionate approach to understanding the gendered impacts of anxiety, worry, and stress—*and* navigating those struggles with vulnerability, strength, and vitality in ways that are fiercely female. I highly recommend this book to anyone who identifies with the pressure to have and do it all, *or else*."

—**Emily K. Sandoz**, Emma Louise LeBlanc/BORSF Endowed
Professor of Social Sciences at the University of Louisiana at Lafayette,
and coauthor of *Living with Your Body and Other Things You Hate*

"*Be Mighty* is an empowering guide to living with more joy and courage. Stoddard writes with a refreshing mix of compassion and humor. Every chapter is peppered with ideas and strategies that have the potential to change readers' lives."

—**Kelly McGonigal, PhD**, author of *The Joy of Movement*,
The Upside of Stress, and *The Willpower Instinct*

"*Be Mighty* by Jill Stoddard is mindfulness and acceptance for the post-#metoo woman. It's chock-full of anecdotes written in an informal language that grabs your attention right from the start. It validates current gender disparities through intelligent and witty repartee—all of which aim to help the reader live a full, vital, and self-compassionate life, without the need for *bulletproof bracelets* à la Wonder Woman. It's acceptance and commitment therapy (ACT) in a nutshell, made easy and yet not oversimplified, adapted to the currently evolving gender identity context. It's just the right length and tone for those of us juggling self-care, work, family, and life!"

—**Jacqueline Pistorello, PhD**, licensed psychologist;
director at University of Nevada, Reno Counseling Services;
and coauthor of *Finding Life Beyond Trauma*

"Constantly battling worry, anxiety, insecurity, and self-criticism is physically exhausting and emotionally draining. Even worse, the attention and effort we invest in keeping up the fight leaves us with little time and energy for the relationships and activities that matter most. *Be Mighty* is an inspiring and empowering guide that offers women a way to disengage from their ongoing battles with fear and anxiety, and bring purpose and meaning to their daily lives. Drawing from evidence-based methods for treating anxiety, Stoddard offers women the practical advice and support they need to harness their inner courage and live boldly and fully."

—**Susan M. Orsillo**, professor of psychology at Suffolk University,
and coauthor of *Worry Less, Live More*

"*Be Mighty* is a call to arms for all women! Reading this brilliant book was like sitting down to a glass of wine with your best friend. Jill is all at once every woman's longtime companion, biggest cheerleader, and tell-it-to-you-straight champion. This is much more than a self-help book for anxiety—it's a compassionate manual for how to navigate the ever-evolving challenges of being a woman in the modern age."

—**Jamie R. Forsyth, PhD**, licensed psychologist, and
international ACT workshop leader

"If you want a book that reads like the author is in the room with you, exuding warmth, compassion, and humor while tackling the complexities of anxiety, then *Be Mighty* is for you. Jill Stoddard offers lots of down-to-earth, practical ideas to give us hope and relief amidst a very troubled world. *Be Mighty* offers simple yet powerful ways to help us identify what matters most, and experiential acceptance and mindfulness practices to help us take anxiety out of the drivers' seat. *Be Mighty* is an empowering, practical, and essential book for women of all ages."

—**Sheri Turrell, CPsych**, clinical psychologist, and owner of Life
in Balance Therapy in Toronto, ON, Canada; adjunct lecturer in
the department of psychiatry at the University of Toronto; Association
for Contextual Behavioral Science (ACBS) peer-reviewed ACT trainer;
and coauthor of *ACT for Adolescents*

"Jill Stoddard offers women a true gift in *Be Mighty*—an accessible set of strategies we can employ to manage the overwhelm of worry and stress inherent in our modern age. Jill's humor, compassion, authenticity, and wise insights offer a guide that is practical and accessible, and which open us up to new opportunities for living well. It's just what every woman needs to become her mightiest self."

—**Yael Schonbrun, PhD**, assistant professor at Brown University
and cohost of the *Psychologists Off The Clock* podcast

"Whimsical and wise in equal measure, this fresh perspective on ACT identifies and addresses the unique hurdles women face while experiencing worries, fears, stress, and anxiety. I highly recommend this to both practitioners and clients alike."

—**M. Joann Wright, PhD**, founder of ACT One;
peer-reviewed ACT trainer; ACBS fellow; and coauthor of *Learning ACT for Group Treatment* and *Experiencing ACT from the Inside Out*

"*Be Mighty* is packed full of wisdom and practical exercises to help you understand your anxiety, worry, and stress, and find a way to courageously connect to and become who you've always dreamt of being."

—**Aisling Leonard-Curtin, MSc, CPsychol, PsSI**,
chartered psychologist with the Psychological Society of Ireland;
codirector of Act Now Purposeful Living; and coauthor of the *Irish Times* #1 bestseller, *The Power of Small*

"If you're a woman, take this book home and read it—today—right now. *Be Mighty* provides the foundation for growth and the path to living life to the fullest. Now is the time in history to help women do that. Jill Stoddard takes the reader on a journey deep inside their fears and anxieties, and has them connect with the life of hope and vitality. I loved this book and will be recommending it to many women, those I work with as well as my dear friends and family. If you care about strengthening women, this book is a breath of fresh air and lays a clear path to a mighty life."

—**Louise Hayes, PhD**, clinical psychologist and senior fellow at
The University of Melbourne and Orygen, Centre for Excellence
in Youth Mental Health; ACBS fellow; and coauthor of *The Thriving Adolescent* and *Get Out of Your Mind and Into Your Life for Teens*

"The book you hold in your hands is a gift to women everywhere! In an age of increased stress and unrelenting pressures, this workbook is a must-read. It is filled with concrete, helpful exercises and advice that will change your relationship with your worry and anxiety. Jill Stoddard provides wisdom and warmth as she guides the reader in developing the courage and conviction to face your fears and live your best life."

—**Laura Silberstein-Tirch**, director of The Center for Compassion
Focused Therapy in New York, NY; author of *How to Be Nice to Yourself*; and coauthor of *Experiencing ACT from the Inside Out*

"*Be Mighty* provides accessible, effective guidance to help women live full lives, even as anxiety arises. Readers will find it informative, comforting, and inspiring. Jill Stoddard's clinical wisdom will be of great benefit to everyone who reads this book."

—**Lizabeth Roemer, PhD**, coauthor of *Worry Less, Live More*

"I can't say enough about Jill Stoddard's *Be Mighty*. Helpful metaphors, excellent storytelling, practical tips, and a large helping of humor make this the book easy to read, digest, and apply to real life. If you're a woman who worries—in other words, if you're a woman—you should read this book."

—**Sara Schairer**, founder and executive director of Compassion It—
a nonprofit and global movement inspiring compassionate actions
and attitudes

"*Be Mighty* is a must-read for any woman who wants to break free from self-limiting narratives, and take steps toward emotional freedom and self-empowerment. This book incorporates evidence-based strategies and practical tools to help women live according to their values. It offers a step-by-step guide with concrete methods, including worksheets and exercises to help women recognize their core beliefs (schemas), clarify their deeply held values, overcome the barriers that hold them back, and take actions toward what matters. I highly recommend this book to all women who are ready to break through their hurdles and live authentically."

—**Avigail Lev, PsyD**, psychotherapist, director of the Bay Area
CBT Center, and coauthor of *ACT for Couples, ACT for
Interpersonal Problems,* and *The Interpersonal Problems Workbook*

"I have never read a book that speaks as directly to my experience as a stressed-out woman in today's world. This book will give you a refreshing perspective on how to cope with anxiety and stress, and help you live a vital and meaningful life. *Be Mighty* is short, fun, and useful—which is exactly what a busy woman like me needs in a book!"

—**Debbie Sorensen, PhD**, clinical psychologist at ImpACT Psychology,
Colorado; and cohost of the *Psychologist Off The Clock* podcast

"Every once in a while, a rare book comes along that changes its readers' lives. *Be Mighty* is such a book. Jill Stoddard sets out to empower women with research-supported coping skills for life's hurdles. Not only does she surpass this goal, but she provides groundbreaking strategies that challenge established beliefs on anxiety and stress. Powerful, funny, soulful, and inspiring, Stoddard's book is an entertaining yet deeply empowering journey. This is a must-read primer for all women."

—**Katherine Nguyen Williams, PhD**, clinical professor of psychiatry
at the University of California, San Diego; and coauthor of
Modular CBT for Children and Adolescents with Depression

"I started reading this book on a Monday, and finished it on Wednesday; that's how captivating it was! There are so many highlights in it that I would need a full page, but because of space, I will share the more important ones: Jill does a beautiful job laying out why a book like this is written at this time; she shares the background of it, and from there, takes the reader into the benefits of applying behavioral science to day-to-day living, while tackling the most common hooks—stories, anxieties, worries—that women face nowadays!… I absolutely appreciate Jill's ability to make ACT accessible in plain language. A must-read and a treat to do so!"

—**Patricia E. Zurita Ona, PsyD**, author of *The ACT Workbook for Teens with OCD*; director of the East Bay Behavior Therapy Center; and ACBS fellow

"Nowadays, it seems that taking care of the self is yet another thing women are expected to do perfectly. In *Be Mighty*, Jill Stoddard offers practical, accessible techniques that honor our growth, our discoveries, and our journeys while also helping us discard the overwhelming and unrealistic sociocultural expectation that we must create the perfectly balanced, glossy, Goop-consumed lifestyle for ourselves. Using her direct, to-the-point approach, Stoddard brilliantly blends the ingredients of effective stress management strategies with the spirit of self-activism. The *realness* in *Be Mighty* is the freshest air I've had in a while."

—**Andrea Letamendi, PhD**, psychologist and consultant; and associate director of mental health training for Intervention and Response for Student Resilience and Residential Life at the University of California, Los Angeles

"Mighty good! *Be Mighty* is engaging, empowering, and full of easy-to-follow information and exercises for women from all walks of life. This is the ACT book I have been waiting for to recommend as a stand-alone self-help book or as an adjunct to therapy (by the way, men might like it too!)."

—**Patricia A. Bach, PhD**, psychologist at Carter Psychology Center, past president of ACBS, and coauthor of *ACT in Practice*

"With *Be Mighty*, Jill Stoddard has brought ACT to life in a warm, uplifting, and humorous way, helping women who struggle with stress and anxiety to find their footing on a values-based path. In this book, she invites women into *living fierce*—a courageous step into vitality! A book for all women seeking mightiness."

> —**Robyn D. Walser, PhD**, author of *The Heart of ACT*; coauthor of *Learning ACT* and *The Mindful Couple*; and assistant professor at the University of California, Berkeley

"Jill Stoddard's *Be Mighty* is a bold, motivating, and down-to-earth guide. Stoddard's encouraging prose informs the reader about utilizing ACT, a behavioral therapy she has used for fifteen years. *Be Mighty* empowers us to make profound changes in our routines so we can live more fulfilling, authentic lives, and become magnificently mighty in the process!"

> —**Dyane Harwood**, author of *Birth of a New Brain*

Be Mighty

A Woman's Guide to Liberation from **Anxiety, Worry & Stress** Using Mindfulness & Acceptance

JILL A. STODDARD, PhD

New Harbinger Publications, Inc.

Publisher's Note

This publication is designed to provide accurate and authoritative information in regard to the subject matter covered. It is sold with the understanding that the publisher is not engaged in rendering psychological, financial, legal, or other professional services. If expert assistance or counseling is needed, the services of a competent professional should be sought.

Distributed in Canada by Raincoast Books

Copyright © 2019 by Jill A. Stoddard
       New Harbinger Publications, Inc.
       5674 Shattuck Avenue
       Oakland, CA 94609
       www.newharbinger.com

Cover design by Amy Shoup

Acquired by Catharine Meyers

Edited by Marisa Solis

Library of Congress Cataloging-in-Publication Data on file

Printed in the United States of America

21   20   19

10 9 8 7 6 5 4 3 2 1   First Printing

To Scarlett, my brave girl.

Keep using your voice.

Mommy will always, always have your back.

Contents

Introduction

You were never Red Riding Hood.

You were always the Wolf.

There is a wolf inside of every woman. Her wolf is who she was made to be before the world told her who to be. Her wolf is her talent, her power, her dreams, her voice, her curiosity, her courage, her dignity, her choices—her truest identity.

—Abby Wambach, *Wolfpack*

Is it just me, or does it feel like life is getting harder? If you're reading this book, you're probably with me on this one. Kids, friends, partners, work, school, finances, health, technology, to-do lists, mass shootings, sexism, racism, homophobia, politics, a constant bombardment of information reminding us how troubled the world is, how little control we have, and how slowly the wheels of change turn. There's not enough Calgon in the world to sufficiently take us away. It can all feel pretty overwhelming.

Even more so when living with anxiety.

Anxiety disorders are the most common psychological complaint, with one in three Americans (Kessler et al. 2005) and 264 million people worldwide (World Health Organization 2017) suffering from an anxiety disorder at some point in their lives. As women, we are about *twice as likely* as our male counterparts to suffer from an anxiety disorder in any given twelve-month period (Kessler et al. 2005). In some ways, the gender gap in anxiety prevalence still shocks me; perhaps it shocks you too. In others, it makes perfect sense. Because research has shown, as women:

- We are paid less than men for doing the same jobs (Bishu and Alkadry 2017).

- We are less likely than men to be introduced by our professional titles (Files et al. 2017).

- We encounter more roadblocks to professional advancement than men (Joshi, Son, and Roh 2015).

- We are bombarded with and negatively impacted by images of how we are expected to appear (tall, thin, fashionable, perky breasts, no cellulite, perfect skin, natural) (Grabe, Ward, and Hyde 2008).

- We take on more of the family and domestic responsibilities, even when we work outside the home (Pew Research Center 2015).

- We are highly likely to be sexually harrassed or assaulted at some point in our lives, and young girls are twice as likely to be sexually abused than young boys (Black et al. 2011; Finkelhor et al. 1990).

- We are evaluated as less competent when we are seen as likable; when we are considered competent, we are more likely to be labeled unlikable (Heilman et al. 2004; Rudman and Glick 1999).

- We speak up less when men are in the room (Karpowitz, Mendelberg, and Shaker 2012).

- We are punished for expressing anger, while men are rewarded (Brescoll and Uhlmann 2008).

- We are seen as less desirable when we outperform men (Park, Young, and Eastwick 2015).

- We pay more for store products when they are marketed toward women compared with identical products marketed toward men, a.k.a. "the pink tax" (De Blasio and Menin 2015).

- We are expected to take on more nonpromotable tasks at work that have little visibility or impact on professional evaluation and advancement (Babcock et al. 2017).

- We are punished more harshly than men for making mistakes, especially in traditionally male occupations (Brescoll, Dawson, and Uhlmann 2010).

Great Rosie's rivet guns! It's a tough world for women. So it's no wonder we struggle with the pain of anxiety, worry, and stress. And let's face it, technology doesn't help. Social media is a breeding ground for social comparison. More than ever, we are checking our standing against the group and worrying that we don't measure up. It can feel, at times, like everyone else has some special key to life—knowing what to say, how to succeed, and how to be confident, stress-free, and happy—but somehow, we were absent on the day those keys were handed out.

So here we are with all of this. Feeling incapable when we struggle with anxiety while the other moms show up to school with Pinterest cupcakes. Feeling inadequate when our totally zenned-out yoga teacher sponsors international refugees in her spare time. The only conclusion to be made is that something is wrong with us. That we are damaged. Broken. Because we have too much pain: we feel anxious, we are worrywarts, we are overly stressed.

We are told and often believe that we are supposed to be Superwomen who can juggle it all calmly, confidently, and unruffled. So we consume books and blogs and podcasts to figure out how to wrangle inner peace with our golden lassos and deflect stress with our bulletproof bracelets in an effort to be those totally together Wonder Women. We only get this one life, after all, so we better make the most of it, and that can't possibly happen if we are damaged and broken and anxious, right? Not quite.

WHAT IF ANXIETY ISN'T THE PROBLEM?

Are we broken? Actually, yeah. Show me a human who doesn't know struggle and pain, and I'll show you that you've traveled to the Land of Make Believe. Our lives literally begin in pain: we come out of the womb screaming (and if we're not, it means something is terribly wrong!). Every single one of us knows how it feels to be rejected or criticized or abandoned, to make mistakes, to fail, to be in the wrong, to be wronged (don't let social media brainwash you into believing otherwise). We accrue a lifetime of hurts that culminate in us being imperfect, "broken" beings. And maybe you've read books or talked with therapists or friends who try to reassure you that you're not damaged, who try to teach you to change your perspective, to build your self-esteem.

I'm not here to do that. Because here's the thing: *maybe it's okay to be broken.* Broken bones heal, but the fracture lines remain permanently visible on X-ray, and we still ache when it rains. But we carry on with our lives, scars and all. Wouldn't it be liberating to just own our brokenness? Shoot, I'm broken. Big time. *And* I live an amazing, full, meaningful life. With all the pain, anxiety, worry, and stress that naturally come with it.

If you're still reading and haven't tossed this book in your "this author lady wears banana pants" bin, then what I'm trying to say here is that maybe anxiety, worry, and stress aren't the bad guys. Pain, whether physical or emotional, communicates to us. The physical pain we feel when we touch a hot stove provides pretty important information, telling us to remove our hand in order to prevent a dangerous burn. Emotions such as fear and anxiety *can* signal a similar need to pull back or avoid. But we often misread our emotional messages.

Because we humans don't particularly like emotions that hurt (and Superwomen are supposed to be able to control them!) we tend to work very hard to prevent, avoid, or escape their discomfort. You might be thinking, *Well, yeah, duh!* I'm certainly not suggesting that there is some glory in feeling pain for the sake of feeling pain. However, we have developed an idea that painful emotions are "bad," that they mean something is "wrong" that needs to be fixed.

Certainly, if you touch the hot stove, the pain does tell you to pull your hand away from that particular burner and to not touch it again until it is no longer hot. But would you disable the entire stove? Bring the whole darn thing down to the recycle center? Maybe to be extra safe, just give up cooking or even avoid kitchens altogether? Of course, this seems ridiculous, because we know these measures are not necessary to prevent another hand burn. Yet this is often exactly what we do when it comes to emotional pain.

Let's dig into this idea using your own personal experience. Bring to mind a difficult past event or series of events in your life that caused anxiety, fear, anger, hurt, worry, or self-doubt. Maybe an important person criticized or even abused you, a romantic partner cheated on you, a close friend let you down, you were the victim of an assault or a car accident, or you experienced sexism or harrassment. Try to make contact with the thoughts and feelings you experienced when this occurred. You hurt! Maybe a lot.

Now think about what happened afterward. Maybe what is still happening. Have you worked hard to stuff the memories and prevent more pain? After the car accident, did you stop driving on the freeway or give up driving altogether? Following the affair, did you withhold your trust from other people and romantic partners?

Chances are, if you had a tough experience, you didn't just learn that one specific person, place, or situation was dangerous or to blame. You likely changed your behavior across people, places, or situations to protect yourself from being hurt again. And here's the real kicker—if you stop driving or dating, you can't crash or get cheated on—so the avoidance "works" to give you a sense of safety and control. You learn that the path to comfort is through avoidance. But at what cost?

Now, maybe instead of being the fierce woman you truly wish to be, you are a version of that woman who is driven by anxiety, worry, doubt, or a powerful need to feel safe. Perhaps you're a woman who thinks, *I'm damaged* or *I'm broken* and allows that narrative to limit her life. If this is the case, you are probably a frequent flier at the popular hot spot known as the Comfort Zone. You know the place—where everything feels familiar and you never have to feel vulnerable, where you feel at ease and have a sense of predictability and control.

The Comfort Zone is cozy. But it is never where the magic happens. Consider a time when you experienced an intense positive emotion, like that intoxicating feeling you get when you're reunited with someone you love. What *necessarily* had to come before that feeling? Answer: the pain of missing him or her so much it hurt.

The pride and satisfaction of winning the award, earning the promotion, or making it to graduation aren't fully felt without also experiencing the longing or fear along the way. I'd be willing to wager that the most powerful and meaningful changes that have occurred in your life thus far have never sprung from you chillin' in your Comfort Zone. For me, this book—which is incredibly important to me—bloomed from an immensely painful experience with a once-respected colleague, coupled with feelings of powerlessness around #MeToo, #TimesUp, and the Christine Blasey Ford congressional hearings. This book would not exist if I had been on holiday in the Comfort Zone.

All emotions—the ones we like and the ones we think we'd rather do without—have purpose and value. If we had no anxiety, we wouldn't study for exams, prepare for presentations, or care for our kids. Most of all, emotional pain is a neon arrow pointing directly at what we care about most. If we didn't care, there would be no reason for it to hurt.

Go ahead and check in with yourself on this one. Think about the last time you had trouble sleeping because of all the worries swirling in your head. Were you fretting about whether Netflix will be able to sustain its production of binge-worthy television? You might enjoy discovering the next great series, but I bet you're not losing sleep over whether that gravy train will end—less care, less pain.

So what *were* you worrying about? The people, animals, or career you love, perhaps? Maybe you were worrying about not being able to sleep. But why? What might happen if you are overtired? Will it impact those people, animals, or career you love? Check your worry spots and I guarantee you'll find the arrow.

HOW THIS BOOK WILL MAKE YOU MIGHTY

Be Mighty is your guide to discovering what deeply matters to you and the fierce woman you might become—a.k.a. "the Me you want to be"—if pain, anxiety, worry, stress, and all the rest of it were no longer holding you back. As you think about "the Me you want to be," consider the following questions:

What might you be doing differently if you weren't listening to the voice that tells you everyone else has it together and you don't measure up?

Who might you be if fear of negative evaluation or rejection wasn't in the driver's seat of your life?

What would you stand for if whats-ifs and fear of uncertainty didn't inhibit you?

What might your life look like if you cast off the suit of armor that makes you feel safe but restricts your ability to freely move around your life?

Be Mighty is here to help you answer these questions, own your scars, and start taking steps in new directions toward becoming your best, boldest, most authentic (and proudly broken!) self. *Be Mighty* will help you identify and become the Me you most deeply desire to be.

Be Mighty is based on the principles of *acceptance and commitment therapy* (ACT; Hayes, Strosahl, and Wilson 1999). ACT (pronounced like the word "act") is a model of psychotherapy whose aim is to improve *psychological flexibility*, or the ability to contact the present moment more fully (including all thoughts, emotions, memories, sensations, and urges, no matter how difficult), and choose actions that are in line with deeply held personal values (Hayes, Strosahl, and Wilson 2012). The goal of ACT is not to feel better but to choose better. To do better. To live better.

Anxiety is on the rise, with a 15 percent increase worldwide over the past decade (World Health Organization 2017). Thankfully, research studies support ACT as a powerful tool to reduce suffering and improve lives for individuals struggling with anxiety (Arch et al. 2012; Eilenberg et al. 2016; Forman et al. 2007; Ritzert et al. 2016; Roemer, Orsillo, and Salters-Pedneault 2008). And people seem to really connect with ACT. I personally live and love ACT, and my clients connect with it too. In at least one research study, participants rated ACT with greater satisfaction than traditional cognitive behavioral therapy (Wetherell et al. 2011).

Gender Sensitivity

Of note, *Be Mighty* uses she/her/hers pronouns. While the hope and intention are for the concepts in this book to apply to both cisgender women (women whose gender identity matches their sex assigned at birth) and to trans*, non-binary, and gender nonconforming people, it is written by a cis-gender woman whose lens may be inadvertently biased.

One of my most deeply held values is to be inclusive and affirming. Another is ongoing personal growth and learning, especially in the realm of cultural sensitivity. In that spirit, I invite trans*, nonbinary, and gender nonconforming individuals and allies to reach out to me personally if there are ways you feel future writings could be more sensitive, affirming, and inclusive.

What You Can Expect in This Book

Be Mighty redefines what it means to be a fierce woman by helping you identify what is truly important to you: who and how you want to be—the Me you want to be—as you navigate this challenging life. You will:

- Become more aware of your anxious thoughts and feelings, especially insofar as they act as obstacles to living the life you want

- Learn to identify connections between your thoughts and feelings and the actions (or inactions) you choose

- Discover the function your behaviors serve—how your chosen actions help you in the moment (and they do, or you wouldn't choose them!)—and the costs at which they may come

- Learn to change your relationship to anxiety and other emotions so they no longer hold you back from being your best self and living your best life

- Learn to make new choices so that life is characterized by greater meaning, vibrance, and might

This book is divided into ten relatively brief and to-the-point chapters (because as women who are expected to juggle it all, who has time to read a long and wordy book?!) based on the core concepts of ACT. Throughout each chapter, you will find metaphors and experiential exercises that will help you internalize and apply what you're learning by transforming words on the page into practices that will bring you into closer contact with your own personal experience. You will also have access to free, downloadable audio recordings to enhance these practices; they are available at http://www.newharbinger. com/34413. The chapters are broken down as follows:

Chapter 1, "Amplifying Your Anxiety Acumen," gets the ball rolling with foundational information about anxiety, worry, fear, stress, and their so-called disorders.

Chapter 2, "Shedding the Shackles of Anxious Avoidance," focuses on the experience of anxiety and the drive to avoid it. We explore the idea that "what we resist persists"—that pain is a universal part of being human, whereas suffering comes from attempts to avoid pain.

Chapter 3, "Cultivating Might Through Mindfulness," focuses on present-moment awareness as a means to cultivate space from where conscious, deliberate, values-driven choices can be made. With mindfulness, we kick autopilot out of the cockpit and reclaim the yoke.

Chapter 4, "Wielding the Weapon of Willingness," presents an alternative to avoidance: developing a willing "bring it on" relationship with whatever internal experiences—your thoughts, emotions, and sensations—happen to come your way.

Chapter 5, "Declaring Victory Through Values," is centered around values identification—defining the life you want and the qualities of being and doing that truly matter to you. Values are "the Me you want to be" and are the heart of being mighty.

In chapter 6, "Understanding Your Suit of Armor," we explore the influence of the past on your present. We identify your protective patterns and evaluate their risk-to-reward ratio.

Chapter 7, "Casting Off Your Suit of Armor," provides guidance for shedding unhelpful habits in exchange for a values-driven life. This includes disengaging from thoughts by becoming a curious observer of the mind.

Chapter 8, "Finding Force in a Fresh Self," explores the concept of self and teaches psychologically flexible responses to self-stories and your inner critic. Self-compassion is included here.

Chapter 9, "Charging Toward Your Best You," focuses on making the mighty moves—"walking the talk"—toward becoming your fiercest self. Overcoming obstacles is highlighted here.

Chapter 10, "Living Fierce: The Finale," pulls everything together by summarizing and connecting concepts with a continued focus on applied practice. This chapter is extra special because it also includes inspiring personal stories from real women who have grown mightier with ACT.

EXPERIENTIAL PRACTICE IN ACT

Humans have amazing brains (especially women, am I right, ladies?) that allow us to think and use language. Unfortunately, language sometimes gets us in trouble. I'm not talking about the language trouble that lands a portion of your paycheck in a swear jar. I'm talking about language creating rules, predictions, judgments, and comparisons (such as, "I'm broken") that alter our experience of the world and can lead to suffering. Let's look at a quick example.

Imagine that I'm sitting next to you with a portable green chalkboard, and to get your attention I take my long fingernails and scrape them down the board. Are you cringing with your shoulders up at your ears? Do you have physical goose bumps? Notice there is no actual chalkboard with you right now. All you had to do was *think* about that chalkboard and you had a physical and emotional response.

The point here is that you had a response to reading the words "nails on a chalkboard" that influenced you in the absence of any direct experience with a chalkboard *in this moment*. Now, of course, you have likely had past experiences with nails on chalkboards. And you might argue, "But nails on chalkboards really are awful and should be avoided when possible!" Fair enough. But there are still no chalkboards with you in this moment.

What if you decided, right now, to stop reading this book or to drop out of school or wear ear plugs to your next lecture, because the language of your mind was telling you nails on chalkboards are just too awful and unbearable?

Similarly, when we have thoughts such as, *I feel like my friends don't think I'm fun* or *My colleagues will think my new ideas are stupid* or *What if this headache is a sign of a terminal illness?* we often respond to those thoughts as Truths (with a capital T!), even though none of those things are actually occurring in the moment. So we miss out. We skip girls' night out instead of connecting with other women, we keep our ideas to ourselves instead of contributing as bold team members, or we spend too much time on WebMD or at the doctor's office instead of spending time with our families or friends.

Have we had a painful past experience that may have fueled the worry? Sure, maybe we have (but not necessarily). And regardless, no painful experience is occurring in this present moment. We overrely on language (thoughts, predictions, rules, assumptions, and the like), make a beeline for our favorite stool at the Comfort Zone, and suffer as a result.

ACT suggests that getting caught up in the language is what causes *psychological inflexiblity*—allowing anxious thoughts and feelings to dominate our choices even if those choices are incongruent with the lives we want. The goal of ACT, then, is to reduce suffering by building greater *psychological flexiblity*—the willingness to show up to the present moment, with whatever happens to exist inside the skin in that moment, and do what matters. In other words, can you have the thought "My colleagues will think my new ideas are stupid" *and* feel anxious about that possibility *and* still share your ideas, because having a voice and being brave are really important to you?

Now, if language causes inflexibility, and you are reading a book to address said inflexibility, and a book is *all language*, how on earth will that work to build flexibility? The way we circumvent the problems of language in ACT is through *experiential learning*.

The Antidote to Inflexible Language Is Experience

An absolutely critical element of ACT is *experiential learning.* Your deepest understanding will not come from reading the information I share as an "expert" (banana pants and all), it will emerge from you connecting the ideas to your own personal experience. You will find metaphors and experiential exercises throughout this book that provide the conduit for making those connections. Of course, these are still presented as words on a page—language—but you will see how language, in the proper context, can connect you to your experience rather than solely serve the role of prediction, comparison, worry, or straight-up-mean-girl self-talk.

In some cases, metaphors will be sprinkled into the text with the intention of bringing concepts to life and making them more salient. In others, you will see sections with the heading "Bring It On." This announces an opportunity to link the reading to your experience. You will need a journal (either paper or digital) in which you can respond to these prompts. Gurrrl, do not skip these! Experiential practice will help you sidestep the problems of language so that you can successfully build psychological flexibility. Basically, bring it on, be a badass.

WHO THIS BOOK IS FOR

If anxiety has you feeling stuck, this book is for you. You want to let go of the things that are holding you back from being your best self or living your best life. You are longing to learn to make new choices so that life is more fulfilling. If you are willing to feel anxiety and other difficult feelings so that you can live out loud, you are likely to benefit from this book. Whether you are a woman who suffers from a diagnosed anxiety disorder or you just feel stuck in life or at work or in relationships, this book can help guide you toward the mighty life you want.

If you are looking for another book to tell you how to get rid of anxiety and find the key to ultimate happiness, this book is not for you.

We are going to dig deep and feel feelings. You will *not* learn how to control, avoid, or "fix" the anxious feelings you don't want. Nor will you learn how to have more of the feelings you do want. Instead, you will learn to change your *relationship* to anxiety so it no longer holds you back.

Living the lives we want—with deeper human connections, more fulfilling work lives, better sex lives, greater adventures—means taking risks. Taking risks means being willing to experience anxiety and feelings of vulnerability. If you are willing to feel all the feels in exchange for a better life, this book is for you. This is what it means to be mighty.

Chapter 1

Amplifying Your Anxiety Acumen

You have to have fear in order to have courage.
I'm a courageous person because I'm a scared person.

—Ronda Rousey

Anxiety is no fun. It's like having your brain hijacked by the Emergency Broadcast System. One minute you're minding your own business, watching your favorite show, and the next that piercing tone! But instead of reassurance that "This is only a test," you're hearing, "This is a very serious warning—we're talking DEFCON 5 here—from the Potential-Emergency Broadcast System. Something could go dreadfully wrong—like extinction-level-event wrong—at any moment, for any reason. And you definitely don't have the chops to deal with it. So, girl, get ready!"

The constant streaming content from the inner Potential-Emergency Broadcast System, or PEBS, is kind of impressive in its magnitude, creativity, and believability (I mean, the powerlines in my backyard really *could* be mutating my cells, right?). Even if the inner PEBS goes quiet for a short time, it's not long before she's transmitting, "So you think you have nothing to worry about? Well, things may seem fine now, but that just means the other shoe is about to drop. Obviously."

Bring It On: Your Inner PEBS

Can you relate to this? Pause for a moment and listen to your inner PEBS. When she sounds the alarm, what types of potential catastrophes does she warn you to watch out for? Write these down in your journal.

If you're asking, "Journal? What journal?" flip back to the Introduction and read the brief section titled "The Antidote to Inflexible Language Is Experience." Remember, experiential practice isn't optional if you truly wish to live a mightier life. If you're not willing to actively engage with the material, you might as well be reading the far less popular book, *Be Meager*.

What you write down in your journal for this exercise will tell us a bit about the specific types of anxiety or fear you tend to experience. Importantly, it will also tell us something about what matters to you (remember that neon arrow?). We will return to these messages in later chapters to investigate how your response to them impacts what matters to you and to learn new, mightier ways of responding when they sound the alarm.

ANXIOUS OR AFRAID?

Anxiety can rear its unsightly head in a number of ways. By simple definition, anxiety is a state of future-focused readiness to deal with potential unpleasant events; this is related to but different from *fear*, which is a more acute reaction to an in-the-moment perceived threat (Barlow 2002). Put another way, *fear* is what we feel when suddenly confronted by a liger; anxiety is what we feel when a liger might be lurking around the corner up ahead. *Worry* is the thinking that arises with anxiety ("What if there's a liger up around that bend?")

The Disney Pixar movie *Inside Out* features a character named Fear who represents both fear and anxiety in the brain of the human protagonist, Riley. If you haven't seen this movie, I highly recommend watching it. You will see excellent (and funny!) examples of fear, such as when Fear responds to Riley's in-the-moment experience of hearing mystery sounds in the darkness of her new bedroom and reacting by immediately assuming it must be a bear (despite being in downtown San Francisco). When Fear is asked for a list of possible negative outcomes on Riley's first day at a new school, he hilariously depicts *anxiety* by asking how to spell the word "meteor." Nothing unpleasant has yet happened to Riley, but Fear is anxious about everything that *could* go wrong over the course of the upcoming day—including meteors!

Your body can probably expertly school you on the myriad physical sensations that also accompany fear and anxiety. We have our sympathetic nervous system, or fight-or-flight response, to thank for fear sensations such as a racing heart, shortness of breath, and lightheadedness. Anxiety sensations typically include gems such as headaches, muscle tension, GI distress, or trouble sleeping.

Stressing the Difference Between Anxiety and Stress

So what is the deal with stress and anxiety anyway? Are they the same? Related? Different? Stress and anxiety share some overlapping physical symptoms, but they are distinct concepts. *Stress* is a response to a specific situation that typically subsides once that situation is no longer front and center (like an upcoming move or job transition). *Anxiety* is more diffuse and lingers even as circumstances change (you've settled into the new house but experience ongoing worry about whether you bought the "right" house or chose the best neighborhood or should have even bought a house in the first place). You might think of stress as a state in which you are prepared for action, whereas anxiety is a state in which you are prepared for (perceived) danger (Marks and Nesse 1994).

So what causes stress? We often blame situations—even the phrase "stressful situation" is a common one. But situations themselves don't cause stress. Take a moment to think of something that stresses you out but does not cause stress to someone you know. If "stressful situations" *caused* stress, we would all experience them in exactly the same way! For example, my husband feels quite stressed driving behind people he perceives to be poor drivers. I, on the other hand, do not find this experience particularly stressful. I *do* feel stressed whenever I'm running late, whereas my husband couldn't care less about punctuality (the heathen!) This is because stress stems from our *appraisal* of situations (Lazarus 1991), not the situations themselves. Specifically, stress refers to whether we see a situation as a *threat* and, if so, how well we believe in our ability to *handle* it.

Let's say you are assigned a big project at work or school. If you do not perceive this as threatening ("No biggie!"), you won't be stressed. If you see it as threatening ("This could make or break me!") and you don't believe in your ability to cope with it ("There's no way I can do this—I'm going to bomb!"), you will be very stressed. If you see a threat ("This could make or break me!") but believe you have what it takes to deal with it effectively ("But I know my stuff and I've worked well under pressure before"), the stress response may be there but will be tempered.

WOULD YOU WIZARD THE WORRY AWAY?

I'm guessing you have wished your anxiety, fear, or stress away on more than one occasion. If I told you this book came with a secret compartment containing a magic wand capable of removing *all* your pain—anxiety, fear, worry, stress, physical sensations—would you wave the wand and chant the magic spell to take it all away? Why or why not? It may sound tempting, but can you think of any reason this might be a terrible idea?

Anxiety has a purpose! As do our other emotions. Anxiety is what motivates us to prepare for the important job interview, watch over our small children, and get pumped up for the big game. What would happen if you had zero anxiety in these situations? You'd be like, "It's all good, I can just wing it, everything will be cool, yo." And you'd likely bomb the interview, lose your kid at the mall, and blow the game.

As it turns out, there is an optimal arousal zone when it comes to doing well (Yerkes and Dodson 1908): when anxiety is very high *or* very low, it has the potential to negatively impact performance. But a moderate level of anxious arousal? That's where it's at.

Similarly, stress has been wrongfully getting a bad rap (McGonigal 2013). While stress does release adrenaline, it also releases oxytocin, the bonding hormone that enhances empathy and motivates us to seek and give care. Oxytocin is a natural anti-inflammatory—it's good for our bodies and actually strengthens our hearts. And, fascinatingly, all we have to do to mitigate the negative effects of adrenaline is simply *appraise* stress as helpful—which you will be well equipped to do by the end of this chapter.

At an individual level, our anxiety, worry, stress, and other emotional pain have purpose in their ability to tell us what we care about most. If we didn't care, there would be no pain. If you look back at your first journal entry ("Your Inner PEBS"), what do you notice? What do your worries tell you about what matters to you? About what you long for? What you don't want to lose? I'm guessing you didn't write a bunch of stuff about your disappointing Candy Crush Saga scores.

And fear? Fear is our friend. Imagine stepping off a curb, looking to your right, and seeing a huge eighteen-wheel truck barreling down the road, coming straight for you. I sure hope you opted out of that magic spell! Fear is what drives us to fight or flee in the face of danger (hopefully yours tells you to flee rather than fight that big truck!).

Elegant Evolution

Humans were programmed with the primitive gift of fear to maximize survivability. And how's this for cool? Every single physiological symptom of fear (or panic) appears to have an evolutionarily adaptive purpose (Cannon 1929). For example, blood is redirected from the extremities to the large muscles and vital organs, causing pale skin and cold or shaking hands; the heart works harder to pump blood to the large muscle groups needed to fight or flee; hyperventilation carries more oxygen to the now rapidly circulating blood; sweating cools the body and makes the skin slippery; and so on.

Even the "freeze" response (often reported by victims of assault) appears to have an evolutionarily adaptive purpose. While immobilization may seem incongruous to survival, the freeze response is thought to act much like an automobile brake, only instead of temporarily slowing down the car to avoid a collision, the "freeze brake" temporarily suspends the fight-or-flight response to allow a space for enhanced perception of the threat and preparation to respond accordingly (Roelofs 2017). In situations where the freeze response most commonly occurs—such as with rape, assault, and other interpersonal violence—fighting or fleeing could be *more* deadly than freezing. The freeze brake allows for perception of the presence of weapons (for example) and consideration of the options that will be least likely to result in harm.

And what about fainting? Could this, too, be an evolved survival mechanism? Fainting is similar to freezing in its resulting immobility, but fainting involves a loss of consciousness, which would prevent the heightened perception and preparation that freezing is designed to allow. That same loss of consciousness would also make fighting or fleeing impossible. For these reasons, those of you who worry that you will faint when you experience intense fear or panic can rest your minds at ease. You may feel lightheaded or dizzy because of the changes in breathing and circulation that accompany the fear response, but *panic and fainting do not occur in tandem* and, in fact, involve opposing activation systems (sympathetic versus parasympathetic) that cannot run simultaneously.

There is one special exception to the you-won't-faint rule, and that little unicorn is the evolutionary adaptation of fainting in the presence of blood—otherwise known as the blood-injection-injury (BII) phobia. In the face of attack and injury, fainting dramatically decreases blood pressure, thereby minimizing blood loss and increasing the odds of survival (Barlow 2002). Boom! Another elegant evolutionary adaptation.

So all of this is to say that anxiety and fear are not only normal, they are helpful. Humans are amazing, complex, special creatures (women especially, of course) who are evolutionarily designed to think and feel *for good reason*. So as much as I hate to disappoint you, there is no secret magic wand compartment, and we will not be using this book to cast any "pain, pain go away" spells.

That is not to say, however, that anxiety and fear are never experienced as excessive. From an evolutionary standpoint (Marks and Nesse 1994) anxiety "disorders" are thought to represent extreme forms of otherwise adaptive anxiety and fear, with the different subtypes of anxiety disorder evolving from specific fears that provided a survival advantage of greater protection from the various risks encountered by early humans. For example, the fittest who survived were those who recognized and responded to threats of social exclusion during a time when hunting and traveling alone were far more deadly than moving together as a group.

Social phobia is thought to be an extreme form of this otherwise adaptive anxiety reaction. Agoraphobia is thought to be an amplification of the adaptive apprehension and fear that protected early humans from the many true dangers encountered when they traveled outside their familiar terrain (Nesse 1987). Individuals with anxiety disorders are like cars with oversensitive alarms: the protection system works great, it's just on a hair trigger and responds to input—whether an actual threat or just the wind blowing—indiscriminately.

Bring It On: My Fear Is Dear

Before we move on, let's pause to connect these ideas to your personal experience. In your journal, take a few minutes to reflect on the question of whether you would wizard away your pain if given the magic wand.

Write about some of the ways your anxiety, worry, stress, or fear may be trying to help you (even if it feels as if the emotion is really bad at it). What has it motivated you to do? How has it protected you (or tried to protect you)? What does it tell you about what matters most to you?

Be sure to really give this exercise a go, as it will lay the groundwork for willingness in chapter 4.

A COMMON LANGUAGE

You may be wondering when I'm going to get to the part about whether your anxiety is social phobia or agoraphobia or BII phobia or another diagnosis. Indeed, these diagnostic labels are how anxiety is largely discussed in the mental health field, and the labels can be useful for organizing the variety of ways anxiety, fear, and stress can present.

For our purposes, though, a diagnostic label is neither relevant to nor necessary for living a mightier life. Diagnostic labels fail to highlight the nuanced ways *you* experience *your* anxiety and how this gets in the way of the life *you* want. However, having a common language—which diagnostic labels provide—for talking about different experiences of anxiety can be helpful when you are looking to learn more about anxiety in general, or when you wish to consult an outside professional who will be familiar with the diagnostic terms.

So for the purpose of amplifying your anxiety acumen and providing you with that common language, I will briefly summarize the diagnostic criteria for each of the anxiety disorders as outlined by the *Diagnostic and Statistical Manual of Mental Disorders*, Fifth Edition

(American Psychiatric Association 2013). However, for the remainder of the book, we will not talk about anxiety as a discrete disorder or mental illness. Instead, we will get curious about your individual experience of thoughts, emotions, sensations, and behaviors—how they interact and how this moves you closer to or farther from a mighty life.

And the Categories Are

Currently, there are five main anxiety disorders in adults: panic disorder, agoraphobia, social phobia, specific phobia, and generalized anxiety disorder (GAD). Until recently, obsessive-compulsive disorder (OCD) and post-traumatic stress disorder (PTSD) were also considered anxiety disorders. In 2013, however, they were reclassified into their own separate categories: obsessive-compulsive and related disorders, and trauma- and stressor-related disorders, respectively. Finally, despite having "anxiety disorder" in its name, illness anxiety disorder is technically considered a somatic symptom disorder. Because all eight of these share anxiety, worry, fear, and/or stress as a central feature, they are summarized for you here.

Panic disorder is characterized by recurrent, unexpected panic attacks in conjunction with fear of future panic attacks or their consequences, or a change in behavior due to panic attacks. A panic attack is defined as a sudden rush of intense fear or discomfort that typically peaks within minutes and involves four or more physiological symptoms, including racing heart, shortness of breath, lightheadedness, numbness or tingling, shaking, sweating, chest pain, stomach distress, chills or hot flushes, feelings of unreality or detachment, fear of dying, or fear of losing control or going crazy.

Agoraphobia is characterized by marked fear or avoidance of experiences such as public transportation, enclosed spaces, wide-open spaces, crowds, or being away from home, where escape or help might not be available in the event of a panic attack or other immobilizing or embarrassing symptoms such as incontinence or diarrhea.

Social phobia (also called social anxiety disorder) is characterized by marked fear or avoidance of social situations (those involving one or more other persons) in which anxiety symptoms may be visible to others, or a performance failure may occur, subjecting the individual to ridicule or humiliation.

Specific phobia is characterized by marked fear or avoidance of a specific object or situation such as heights, dogs, enclosed spaces, or needles.

Generalized anxiety disorder is characterized by excessive, uncontrollable worry about a number of different things—like money, school, health, or minor matters—that is accompanied by three or more of the following: feeling keyed up or on edge, fatigue, trouble concentrating, irritability, muscle tension, and trouble sleeping.

Obsessive-compulsive disorder is characterized by time-consuming, intrusive, distressing thoughts, images, or impulses (also known as obsessions) and/or repetitive behavioral or mental acts that are aimed at reducing the distress caused by obsessions.

Post-traumatic stress disorder is characterized by intrusions of repetitive and distressing thoughts, memories, nightmares, or similar; avoidance of trauma-related triggers such as people, places, or situations; reactivity in the form of hypervigilance, exagerrated startle, irritability, and the like; and changes in beliefs and mood, such as self-blame and detachment. All of these symptoms occur as the direct result of a traumatic event in which actual or threatened death, serious injury, or sexual violence were experienced, witnessed, or repeatedly learned about.

Ilness anxiety disorder is characterized by anxious preoccupation with having or acquiring a serious illness, accompanied by excessive reassurance-seeking behaviors such as body checking, medical tests, and doctor visits.

For any of these to "count" as an official diagnosis, they must meet specific time criteria, must "pass" other rule-outs (such as not being due to a medical illness or caused by a substance), and must cause significant distress or impairment at work, school, or in relationships. Interestingly, this assumes "the disorder" itself is the problem.

What I and many others would argue is that the "symptoms" (worry, fear, anxiety, panic) are not actually the problem; rather the unwillingness to have these internal experiences leads to avoidance of what triggers them, which serves to amplify and maintain the symptoms while also restricting life. Said another way, anxiety is not the problem; *avoidance* of anxiety is. Much more on this throughout the book.

SURVIVAL ON STEROIDS

I imagine there's at least a small part of you nodding along with the compelling thesis that anxiety and fear can be adaptive. And there may be another part of you that connects with the excessive or extreme side of anxiety, which is saying, "Helpful, shmelpful! My 'primitive gifts for survival' feel like they're on steroids! I panic like the Hulk! My worry game puts Piglet's to shame! Why? How did I get like this?"

What makes some people more likely to develop problematic anxiety than others? Researchers have been trying to answer this question for decades. It turns out the answer is as complex as we are (and well beyond the scope of this book!). The good news, though, is that we don't need to understand the multifaceted interaction between your biology and learning history to move you toward being mighty. In fact, a hyperfocus on "why" and "how" (sometimes called "intellectualizing") can be a form of avoidance and typically causes problems more than solves them.

Think of yourself like you think of your smartphone or tablet. A lot of very complicated computer programming is required to make your devices work. Do you understand the 1's and 0's that make them browse, text, and talk? Not likely (unless you are a programmer by trade, in which case, you go, girl!). And yet, you plow forward anyway, doing what you need to do to complete assignments, video chat with family, search for hiking trails, and read e-books. You don't try to interpret the code before you move ahead to take effective action.

What we do know is that *experiential avoidance*—an unwillingness to have anxiety (and other inner pain) plus active attempts to prevent or escape it—is at the core of all anxiety disorders (Forsyth and Eifert 1996). For you to grow, get unstuck, and be mighty, we simply need to understand the ways your life is currently limited by experiential avoidance. This will be the topic of the next chapter.

THE TAKEAWAY

Anxiety (future-oriented state of liger readiness), worry (thinking, "what-if liger..." component of anxiety), fear (in-the-moment liger alarm), and stress (appraisal of liger threat and lack of coping resources) can emerge in response to a number of objects (like ligers), events, and situations. Because these experiences can be uncomfortable, we may wish to avoid them. However, our emotions have purpose—both to protect us and to point out what we care about. Unwillingness to experience those emotions, combined with active attempts to suppress them, are at the core of stuckness.

Chapter 2

Shedding the Shackles of Anxious Avoidance

If I stop to kick every barking dog I am not going to get where I'm going.

—Jackie Joyner-Kersee

What is your go-to when you feel anxious, worried, or stressed? Do you like a nice glass of wine, a perfect to-do list, or a creative excuse to get out of a social engagement? Experiential avoidance is an unwillingess to experience anxiety or other uncomfortable internal emotions or sensations, along with active efforts to change, reduce, or eliminate those internal experiences (Forsyth and Eifert 1996).

Avoidance can also come in the form of choices that are designed to prevent a feared or unwanted outcome. For example, let's say you are invited to a party and this triggers worry that you won't know what to say, you won't be interesting, and others will ultimately avoid talking to you. What might you do to feel less anxious or prevent those feared outcomes from occurring? A number of options likely spring to mind: don't attend, attend but drink four margaritas to lower your inhibitions, attend but prepare a list of interesting conversation topics in advance. Will these work to lower anxiety? Prevent the outcomes? Probably. If they didn't work, you wouldn't choose them. Let's investigate.

Bring It On: Taking Inventory

Let's look more closely at your personal experience of anxiety and how you typically respond when it shows up. Bring to mind a recent experience with anxiety. Conjure the thoughts, emotions, physical sensations, and urges you experienced. Then what did you do? Did it work to make you feel better, even if just for a moment? I'll bet my bottle of pinot that it did.

In your journal, make a table with five columns. At the top of the first column, write "Anxiety and other pain." In the second, "Strategies: what I do or don't do." In the third, "Benefits," and in the fourth, "Costs." The last column should be labeled "What does your experience tell you?" (You can also make your life easier by downloading the Avoidance Inventory worksheet at http://www.newharbinger .com/34413.) Now let's complete the table, one column at a time, following these steps:

1. In the first column, list all the internal expeiences you struggle with. These might be things like anxiety, fear, panic, self-doubt, uncertainty, stress, irritability, fatigue, headaches, and others that are similar.

2. When your first list is complete, move on to the second column and list all the things you do or don't do when the internal experiences from column one show up. Don't think about whether your actions are "good" or "healthy" or "bad" or "unhealthy"—just write anything down, without evaluation. These might be things such as deep breathing, medication, socially isolating, napping, snapping at people, avoiding certain situations, drinking alcohol, practicing yoga, making lists, going over and over the pros and cons before making a decision, procrastinating, keeping opinions to yourself, people pleasing, and the like.

3. Now, in the third column, write down the benefits of these strategies, including benefits that seem small

or momentary. These might be things like "feel more calm," "feel in control," "lower inhibitions," "feel more certain"; they will probably all have some element of feeling better or relief in common.

4. In the fourth column, write down the costs of these strategies. Make sure you are focusing on the costs of the *strategies*, not of the pain. These might be things like time, money, damage to my body, damage to my relationships, increase in stress/anxiety, not who I want to be, further from the life I want, and more.

5. Finally, look over the results and write down in the last column what your experience tells you. If you are stuck, try filling in this sentence: Whenever I feel _____ [anxious, uncomfortable, etc.], I do _____ [the behavior] to try to feel better. This gives me _____ [how you feel right away, in the short term, such as "some relief"], but I see that _____ [the long-term result, such as "it makes the situation worse in the long run"].

WILL THE REAL EXECUTIONER PLEASE STAND UP?

Maybe anxiety and other discomfort are not actually the problems. Gasp! Yes, you read that right. What does your experience tell you? Are the costs you identified in your journal really because of your anxiety…or something else?

We are great at making ourselves feel better. In the short term. But there's a catch. The very strategies we employ to feel better today don't work quite as well tomorrow and the day after that. If they did, you wouldn't be reading this book! Maybe anxiety isn't the problem. Maybe the problem is the strategies we employ to "cope" with our anxiety. In

Buddhism, this concept is simplified by the saying *Pain x Resistance = Suffering*. The strategies are resistance. Pain exists, suffering is optional. Let's look at a few common examples.

Procrastination

You have a deadline or a task at home and you just don't feel like you can muster up what it takes to buckle down and get it done. The dread builds until finally you blurt, "Ugh! I don't feel like it [or, 'I can't do it' or 'I shouldn't have to do it' or 'it won't be good enough']. Screw it, I'll just deal with it later."

How do you feel in the very moment you give yourself permission to put off the dreaded task? Relieved, right? *It works, or we wouldn't do it.* And the cost? You have the same stuff to do, plus likely more piled on, and less time to do it. So the dread and anxiety you successfully avoided yesterday are now amplified today.

Procrastination can be a bit like skydiving. You're on a plane that's climbing and you know you have to jump out, but you're dreading it. There's an ideal altitude at which to jump, but you're understandably nervous. So you wait until you feel more motivated to take the leap. But the longer you wait, the higher you climb. You still have to make the jump (assuming you care about getting back on the ground), but the higher you climb, the more nervous you become, the greater the distance you have to fall, and the more you dread the actual dive.

Anxiety and dread often fuel procrastination, and putting off an aversive task feels good temporarily. But ultimately, the anxiety grows, the time you have to jump shortens, and you still have the problem of the incomplete task. Reflect on how this fits with your own experience of procrastination.

Situational Avoidance

You're invited to a girls' night out or assigned a presentation for work or school. You feel anxious, insecure, uncertain. You worry that you'll blow it, that others will see your social incompetence or failure to perform. Your mind starts coming up with excellent excuses for why you can't or shouldn't. So you bow out.

How do you feel in the moment you give yourself permission to avoid the situation? Ahh, there's that sweet relief once again: *It works, or we wouldn't do it.* As long as you don't attend or perform, you can't fail, so you feel better. But at what cost? Chances are, there will be regret around missing out or letting fear dictate important choices. It's also likely that it will be even harder to say yes the next time an invitation arises. By avoiding an anxiety-provoking situation, you gain comfort. But you also forgo all the possibilities that stepping into that situation may have afforded. It's a huge trade-off that risks an increasingly narrow life.

Situational avoidance is like building a brick house (Stoddard and Afari 2014). Every brick house (your life) must contain bricks (your thoughts, emotions, and sensations). You have a pile of these bricks available to you. Upon inspection, you notice that some of the bricks are nicer than others: some of them are clean and new, while others are chipped and dirty.

What would happen if you chose to build your house with only the perfect bricks? It might look pretty, but it sure would be a tiny house! Now, maybe you're thinking you're okay with a tiny house. Tiny houses are more cozy anyway. The thing is, though, that pile of chipped and dirty bricks is still sitting right outside. Every time you step out of your diminutive domicile, the rejected bricks are right there on the path. If you're so turned off by the imperfect bricks, you might reach the point at which you stop leaving the house altogether. That sounds like quite the sacrifice!

What would happen if you chose to build your house with *all* of the bricks you have at your disposal? What if a true dream house is a space where you can choose to be surrounded by bricks that are clean, dirty, old, new, chipped, pretty, perfect, and imperfect in the service of having a bigger life—a life in which there is no limit to your freedom to move about? Reflect on how this fits with your personal experience of situational avoidance.

Giving in to Urges

You're feeling anxious, worried, or full of doubt, and you notice a strong desire to visit all your social media accounts (again), eat the rest of that large pizza, or check the door locks for the fourth time. Cravings and urges, by definition, involve very intense, burning desires for something. Urges may also come with intrusive, unwanted thoughts. It's incredibly uncomfortable. It can even feel unbearable. Tired of discomfort and obsessive thinking, you "get a case of the 'screw-its'" (as one of my former clients liked to say) and give in to the urge.

When you're obsessing about your ex, anxious and insecure, how do you feel as you succumb to the impulse to dive deep into his or her social media account? Probably free. Free from the urges and obsessive thoughts, with some added pleasure from the dopamine sprinkled in. *It works, or we wouldn't do it.* But at what cost?

More than likely, the urge has been replaced by more anxiety and uncertainty as you question who the new girl is in the photos, and possibly shame for giving in (especially when you kind of knew it would ultimately make you feel worse). And it won't be long before those unwanted thoughts and urges return.

Giving in to urges is like feeding a hungry mogwai. One morning, you hear a strange sound outside your door, an incessant high-pitched giggly noise. When you open the door, you see an adorable little fur ball with huge, pleading eyes—it's a magical mogwai! You think, *Poor thing must be hungry, I'll feed her a little snack.* The mini meal stops the noise, and you can't help but invite the cute little bugger inside.

This goes on every day, and you give the mogwai food each time she loudly begs for it. Whenever you feed her, she quiets down and resumes looking adorbs. Until one day, very late at night, she comes begging for another snack. The noise escalates, becoming nearly unbearable. You know feeding her will quiet the cacophony, but you also know the number-one rule of caring for a mogwai is to never, ever, *ever* feed her after midnight. Not wanting to listen to the racket that's keeping you up when you should be asleep, you think, *How bad could one little chicken leg really be?* You give her the snack and this does the trick. She pipes right down and you get a good night's rest.

When morning comes, you hear another strange noise, only this is a sound you haven't heard before. When you emerge from your bedroom, your sweet puffy pet has transformed into an evil gremlin who begins terrorizing you. And you realize the trap you've created— and that if you don't give her what she wants, she might eat you next!

Giving in to urges feeds them, helping the mogwai grow louder and peskier, ultimately becoming a vicious gremlin who controls your life in a seemingly inescapable cycle. Reflect on how this fits with your own experience of giving in to urges.

Lashing Out

You didn't get enough sleep, forgot to eat breakfast, and have a to-do list as long as your arm, with not enough hours in the day to get it all done. As anxiety and irritability build, you mutter annoyances at the barista who has no control over the speed of the espresso machine, send a passive-aggressive text to your partner, and honk at the guy who's still looking at his phone when the light turns green (well, that one might be deserved).

Impulsive reactions feel cathartic and justified, like a moment of vindication and release. *It works, or we wouldn't do it.* But they are just that—momentary. You are left no less stressed than before you lashed out, and you may add to that stress with guilt, regret, or a damaged relationship if your target was someone you care about.

Put another way, lashing out can be like swimming at the beach (Stoddard and Afari 2014). One minute you're having fun and the next you're getting sand in your eyes from the kid shaking off his towel right next to you. You head into the water to rinse off when you're suddenly knocked off your feet and are being pulled out to sea by a rip current. You panic and start paddling furiously against the rip in an effort to get back to shore. You do it without thinking. It's instinctive. But you're getting nowhere—and getting exhausted.

The key here, instead, is to float or swim slowly with the rip or parallel to shore. As you do this, you'll feel the tug of the current and may get carried out farther than you'd like. You'll feel nervous *and* you can float with the rip *while* experiencing those feelings. Eventually, the rip may send you back to shore, or you will come to calm water and be able to swim or walk back to your spot on the beach. Perhaps you can let go of paddling furiously (lashing out) and instead allow the anxiety and irritability that come with things not going as desired to be present while you move in ways that are effective. Reflect on how this fits with your own experience of lashing out.

Passivity

Many women receive subtle and not-so-subtle messages that being female and being assertive is not okay. Asking for what we want or need, setting limits, saying no, or expressing ourselves (especially if the message might be unwanted, heaven forbid!) can lead to worry about being seen as not nice or too needy, aggressive, bossy, or bitchy.

When your heart says, "Speak up," but your fear says, "Shut down," to which do you listen? When fear wins, what happens? Perhaps a sense of safety, at first—*it works, or we wouldn't do it*—but at what cost? Needs go unmet, your authentic self is sacrificed, bitterness and resentment join the team, and passivity may ultimately swing to aggression, damaging the relationships you were trying to protect by being passive in the first place.

It's like trying to submerge a floating ball under the surface of the water (Stoddard and Afari 2014). It takes a lot of effort and energy to shove the ball under the water, and in no time, it's crashing back up through the surface. Similarly, we push down the feelings that show up when we think about having a voice or taking up space, but ultimately they keep popping back up. And the farther down we shove them, the more they explode back through, bringing along added bitterness and resentment that will have to be shoved down too! Struggling with the ball in this way keeps it close by. The battle is tiring and futile. All our energy, effort, and attention are engaged in this struggle, making it difficult to focus on other important things. Reflect on how this fits with your own experience of choosing to be passive.

Grabbing for the Good

Hopefully now you can see that struggling to avoid discomfort can be highly problematic. Similarly, efforts to grab on to pleasant feelings are also futile. The feelings we want—security, a sense of control, confidence, happiness, love—are like one of those toy water snakes. Can you picture it? The rubber tube filled with water? What happens as you grab it? The stronger the squeeze, the more likely the toy snake is to slide right out of your hands. It's not for lack of effort or strength, it's just a rigged game. The snake is not designed to be grabbed. And neither are our feelings. Let's investigate.

Bring It On: Winning Lottery Ticket

How would you like to win the Powerball? You can set the amount you wish to win—not so little that it doesn't make a dent, not so much as to be a burden. All you have to do to claim the winning ticket is feel deeply proud of Ted Bundy for his impressive murder spree. Just conjure a true, authentic, strong sense of pride for Ted. Write in your journal in an effort to help produce this pride and notice how you feel. Could you do it? I sure hope not! And why not? What if the incentive were higher? Still not going to win.

Because no matter how badly you want to feel a certain way, we're simply not built to control our feelings in that way. You might be able to *act* as if you are proud of Mr. Bundy, but you'd be faking the feelings part. You simply can't force yourself to have, or not have, feelings. In fact, I'd be willing to bet my own lottery winnings that the harder you try to conjure that pride in Ted, the more you'd have to think about him and therefore the gruesome details of what he's known for, making the likelihood of feeling pride even more elusive than before I offered you the lotto winnings.

In your journal, reflect on ways you've tried to force feelings you want more of, such as joy, control, confidence, security, or love. Reflect on your "success" and also how these things have eluded you, like pride for Ted or the sliding water snake.

THE ANXIETY TRIUMVIRATE

There are three amigos that add fuel to the anxiety fire. Individuals who struggle with (1) intolerance of uncertainty, (2) a lack of perceived control, and (3) an overinflated sense of responsibility tend to experience greater challenges with anxiety (Barlow 2002). This can be particularly problematic for women, as we often juggle work, school, home, partner, and kids all at the same time.

When you are troubled by the anxiety triumvirate, you will do whatever it takes to get answers and fix the problem, all while staying in charge. This might look like excessive Internet searching (Hello, WebMD, is this headache a migraine?), overinvolvement in kids' lives (Hello, Principal Spencer, can we talk about my son's C in social studies?), reassurance seeking (Hello, spouse, why are you forty-two seconds late? Is everything okay? Are you okay? Are we okay?), or excessive checking (Hello, doors, are you still locked and keeping us safe? How about now? Still locked?).

While these behaviors may provide a sense of comfort in the moment—*it works, or we wouldn't do it*—what do you notice as time goes on? Answer: Greater uncertainty (My headache might be a brain tumor?!), a further diminished sense of control (Why can't I change the teacher/principal/husband's behavior?!), and more pressure to shoulder responsibility (Things are falling apart on my watch, I better double down!). This is a perfect example of how "grabbing for the good" can backfire.

This list of examples could go on and on. Notice what these examples and your personal experience all have in common: *Our responses to distress and discomfort make us feel better temporarily but keep us stuck in the long run*. Don't believe this just because I'm saying it's so. Truly consider what you've written in your journal and how the metaphors have moved you to connect with this in a personally meaningful way: Pain x Resistance = Suffering. Or, as I like to say:

Anxiety x Struggle = Suffering

Anxiety is a universal human experience. It is our struggle to fix, control, or avoid the anxiety that threatens to make an ASS out of us.

WHY WE KEEP FIGHTING

So if this is true, why do we keep doing it? For one, because it works, but you already know that. More specific, though, to say "it works" is to say that all behavior has a function—it serves a purpose. What we've been talking about here is behavior that serves the purpose of making us feel better, giving us relief. We also do it because we think we can. We think we should be able to solve "problems" inside our bodies (uncomfortable thoughts, emotions, sensations, and urges) because our experience solving problems outside our bodies tells us it's possible (Hayes and Smith 2005).

Look around the room you're currently in. Imagine for a moment that the door to this space (assuming you're inside) is suddenly locked and you're trapped inside. What would you do? Take a moment to consider some stategies for solving this problem. Perhaps you think about yelling to someone in the next room, using your mobile phone to call for help, or breaking a window so you can climb out. Or, if you're me, you think about kicking your feet up and enjoying the peace and quiet for a while, and then eventually getting around to all those other things. The point is that you were able to immediately generate a list of viable solutions to the locked-door problem, even if you've never had the experience of being trapped.

If a liger were in the same predicament, she would be in big trouble! Ligers and other non-human species don't have the same amazing cognitive abilities we humans have that allow us to solve complex problems. This is one of the special qualities that places us at the top of the food chain. The problem arises when we attempt to apply these same problem-solving abilities to our inner world. We think that because we can get out of the locked-room dilemma, we should also be able to get out of the anxiety dilemma. *We see uncomfortable thoughts and feelings as problems to be fixed, and we work hard to escape the discomfort, much like we might work to escape from a locked room.*

Unfortunately, problems inside the skin don't work quite the same as problems on the outside. Let's break down the locked-room dilemma. I might be the **SOLVER** of this problem by doing as follows:

State the problem: I tried to exit the room but was unable to do so.

Origin of the problem, as this may provide a solution (for example, if I discovered the reason I was unable to leave the room was a locked bolt, I would just unlock it): The door appears to be stuck because the locking mechanism is broken.

List possible outcomes if no action is taken: Eventually I will starve or dehydrate to death.

Vote for a solution and take action: Yell, bang on door, call someone, break the window if none of the above work.

Evaluate effectiveness: Called maintenance from my cell phone and they got me out.

Recognize the lesson to prevent future problems: I won't shut the door tightly until maintenance has had a chance to fix the broken lock.

This would be a highly effective strategy for solving the locked-door problem *and* for preventing future room stuckness. So let's try applying these problem **SOLVER** steps to solve the "problem" of panic attacks.

State the problem: I had a panic attack at the mall.

Origin of the problem, as this may provide a solution: Uhh…the mall? The crowds? The heat? Being dehydrated? *(Here's problem #1: we usually can't answer this question and will wrongly attribute causes.)*

List possible outcomes if no action is taken: Heart attack, death, losing control, suffocating, fainting. *(Here's problem #2: this will be an unsubstantiated worry.)*

Vote for a solution and take action: Get the heck out of the mall! Deep breathing while walking to the car, call a friend on the way home. If still not better, take a Xanax. *(Here's problem #3: these are arbitrarily chosen or based on "origins" identified above that are likely not accurate.)*

Evaluate effectiveness: My panic attack subsided in about fifteen minutes, so I guess my solution worked. *(Here's problem #4: the panic attack would have subsided in fifteen minutes anyway, but now escape is wrongfully getting the credit.)*

Recognize the lesson to prevent future problems: Stay away from the mall; always carry Xanax, water, and phone, just in case; consider only going on outings with others rather than alone. *(Here's problem #5: psychological inflexibility and huge cost!)*

Here's one more example that demonstrates how attempting to problem-solve anxiety leads to psychological inflexibility:

State problem: Anxious on the way to a party.

Origin of problem: It's because I have no social skills and am boring.

List outcomes if no action taken: I'll get to the party and I'll be humiliated!

Vote and do it: Don't go to the party.

Evaluate effectiveness: Anxiety went away and I wasn't humiliated.

Recognize lesson: Stay away from social situations to prevent anxiety and humiliation.

Bring It On: Feelings SOLVER

Okay, now it's your turn. Choose a feeling (emotional or physical) you work hard to prevent, control, or escape. In your journal, repeat the SOLVER steps outlined above (you can also download and print out this worksheet at http://www.newharbinger.com/34413). Reflect on the "success" or costs of your solutions.

Look at your experience and see if this rings true for you: we might be able to "successfully" solve the "problem" of fear or dread or anxiety temporarily, but ultimately, *the more we try to escape discomfort, the more stuck we become, and it comes back. Every. Single. Time.*

SO IS FEELING BETTER…BAD?

But wait. Is it *always* a problem to make ourselves feel better? Good news…it's not. The question always boils down to two things:

1.   What is this choice (action or inaction) in the service of?

2.   Does it have a cost?

If a behavior is in the service of changing, stuffing, "fixing," or avoiding certain thoughts and feelings, it fits the definition of experiential avoidance. However, not all avoidance is problematic; it depends on its cost.

Take the example of a headache. When I have a headache, I take ibuprofen. Would this be considered experiential avoidance? Does it alter my internal experience? Yes. Is it problematic? Does it come at a cost? Well, if I take 400mg of ibuprofen every so often for acute pain, there isn't much cost. The generic brand isn't terribly expensive and ibuprofen is not known to cause internal damage at low doses. In fact, it might even make it more likely that I say yes to that board game with my kids or dinner party invitation with my friends. *We call behavior that expands our engagement in a rich and meaningful life "workable."*

But what if I'm so unwilling to experience any amount of discomfort (and let's face it, as we start to age something will always hurt a little!) that I take 800mg of ibuprofen (prescription strength) every four hours for many years. Now the avoidance very likely has a cost—to my wallet as well as the lining of my stomach—and, in fact, is very likely now *causing* the exact headaches I've been trying to avoid. *We call behavior that restricts access to a full and vital life "unworkable."*

Bring It On: Consider the Costs

Reflect on the common strategies discussed above and how they fit with your experience. In your journal, write about the costs to you and your life of procrastinating, avoiding situations, giving in to urges, lashing out, and being passive. Write about the unworkability of seeking certainty and control, and of taking on too much responsibility.

Of course, we all engage in experiential avoidance sometimes. And it might even seem like we've gotten pretty good at managing it. But how long does that last before bringing harm to our jobs, our bodies, and perhaps most important, our relationships? *Avoidance is a problem—or unworkable—when it pulls us away from what matters most.*

Trying to control your anxiety with avoidance is like joining the circus to learn how to juggle and hula hoop (Stoddard and Afari 2014). Just about anyone can toss one ball back and forth. Lots of people can even juggle two balls. It's also pretty easy to get a single hula hoop to circle your hips a few times. Similarly, it might seem like your strategies for avoiding your anxious feelings are doable and effective and don't come at much of a cost.

But what happens as you add more balls or hula hoops to your circus act? You have to concentrate more and more to keep things going. In fact, you can hardly concentrate on anything else! After a while, all of those hula hoops restrict your movement and the balls come crashing down on you. Something that started out as simple, doable, and harmless becomes suffocating and impossible to keep up. Reflect on the avoidance you've been juggling. How have you been "successful" up to a point? How have the hoops ultimately restricted you? How have the balls come crashing down?

THE TAKEAWAY

Anxiety is a universal human experience. While it can certainly feel uncomfortable, it is not the enemy (and, as you now know, it can actually be adaptive). Avoidance can give us a temporary sense of control, which can feel mighty in the moment. However, we rarely feel strong for long. Oh no, soon we just feel like an ASS: Anxiety x Struggle = Suffering. No weapon in the world can exterminate anxiety, but there are several we can wield to reduce suffering. Before adding those to your arsenal, we are going to pause and prepare by honing our powers of presence in chapter 3.

Chapter 3

Cultivating Might
Through Mindfulness

*Don't look at your feet to see if you are doing it right.
Just dance.*

—Anne Lamott

Hopefully you have been fully engaging with the experiential material in chapters 1 and 2. If you have not, get in touch with the thoughts and feelings that have contributed to your decision to skip it. What do you get in the moment you give yourself permission to not write in your journal? Relief from the effort or uncertainty of what it's all about? A sense that you're moving forward more quickly (with the hope of having that mighty life even sooner)? Consider the potential cost of that choice in the long run.

If you have been *bringing it on*, way to go! You are already shedding the shackles of avoidance and on your way to a mightier you. When you can understand the importance of avoiding avoidance, the next big question, naturally, is "Great, so now what?" Everything you read in this book is designed to help improve your psychological flexibility. By the end, you should have a very different relationship to your anxiety and many more behavioral options for living the life you truly desire. To make those changes, you must first become a very keen observer.

WHEN AUTOMATIC PILOT TAKES OVER

To start, think about the last time you drove to work or chauffeured your kids to karate or mommy-and-me music class (if you don't drive, think about the last time you were driven). What details did you see, hear, smell, and physically feel?

I bet you're thinking, *Uh, I have no idea.* Unless you nearly crashed, you probably weren't paying much attention to the details of your driving experience. You were more likely replaying a conversation from earlier in the day, planning the dinner menu, or fretting about tomorrow's exam or work meeting. Who, then, *was* driving the car while you were busy revisiting the past and beaming into the future? Enter your autopilot.

In flight, automatic pilot, or *autopilot*, refers to a system that keeps the aircraft flying without direct input from the human aviator. Similarly, we have a psychological version of automatic pilot: it is our muscle memory that takes over and either flies us to and fro, just outside our conscious awareness, or reacts abruptly without thinking or choosing.

Sometimes that autopilot might come in handy. For example, I was recently driving my four-year-old to preschool when my autopilot took over the yoke for the physical journey, freeing up the rest of my awareness to soak in the sounds of my delightful little boy singing a pop song with his adorable lisp, completely out of tune, at the top of his lungs.

But what about when that same little boy isn't being quite so delightful? When it's the end of a long day and he's fighting with his sister or refusing to eat his "dithguthting" dinner (okay, the lisp is always pretty cute)? What happens for you in challenging situations like this? When intense irritability or impatience (or some other powerful emotion) shows up?

More than likely, if your autopilot has commandeered the cockpit, the space between intense emotion and response is utterly nonexistent, leading to an instant, impulsive reaction. It's as if the intense emotion is a detonator and the reaction a bomb. And how often is that bomb—reacting impulsively—going to be in line with the Me you most wish to be? My autopilot drops a nasty snap bomb on my poor, tired kids, which is not even close to being in line with the mom I want to be.

Bring It On: Hijacked!

Before we move on, consider the autopilot in your life. In your journal, describe a personal experience when you got hijacked by your automatic pilot. Note as many relevant details as you can recall by answering these questions:

* What were you doing, who were you with, where were you, what was the time of day?

* How were you feeling emotionally and physically?

* What were you thinking? On when and what were you focused? Did you cognitively time travel to the past or future, or get sucked into a tech device? What was the content of your thoughts?

* What acted as a detonator, and what was the bomb?

* How much space was between the two?

* In what ways did your autopilot support or interfere with the Me you want to be or the life you want to live?

If we want to create an optimal context for mighty living, we need to expand the space between detonator and bomb—between internal experiences and reaction. It is in this space where we can dismantle the bomb through willing, conscious, deliberate choice; where we can decide to respond in accordance with who we want to be and what matters to us most, even when the detonator has been pushed. Our key to unlocking that space is in slowing down and cultivating greater present-moment awareness.

Bring It On: Just One Breath

Anxiety can act like a natural stimulant, speeding up the body, the mind, and the speech, almost to the point of vibration. Notice your own experience of this.

During the next few days, choose an activity, time of day, or interpersonal interaction. Whatever you choose, commit to taking just one breath, slowly and deliberately, before your first action, step, or word. Then, intermittently, take just one breath in between the actions that follow. Allow your breath to slow things down and anchor you in the present, creating a larger space for choice. What do you notice when you do versus don't take just one breath? How does this impact your autopilot?

MINDFULNESS

The concept of *mindfulness* has become increasingly popular and more mainstream (a quick Google search results in more than 135 million hits!). By definition, mindfulness is the practice of "paying attention in a particular way: on purpose, in the present moment, and nonjudgmentally" (Kabat-Zinn 1994, 4).

Mindfulness practice can take the form of sitting on a cushion, in formal meditation, for forty-five minutes, the benefits of which are many. However, if you're like Kimberly "Sweet Brown" Wilkins and me, you're thinking, "Ain't nobody got time for that!" And that's fine. Because "be more mindful" does not need its own spot in your calendar or on your to-do list. Especially if formal mindfulness practices are being scheduled as yet another strategy for reducing anxiety (this should set off alarm bells for you now!).

Purposeful awareness of the present moment can be cultivated by observing the details of our everyday sensory experiences—what we see, smell, hear, taste, and touch—and by noticing the features of our ongoing internal experiences, such as awareness of the breath, mind, and body (thoughts, emotions, images, memories, sensations). We can practice building this awareness without ever sitting on a cushion. We can brush our teeth mindfully, shower mindfully, eat mindfully, interact with others mindfully. We can watch the activity of our minds, observe the tension in our muscles, and notice emotions and urges to act.

Of course, no one is able to stay present 100 percent of the time (not even the Dalai Lama, from what I've heard). Practicing mindfulness means flexibly shifting our attention, choosing to return to the present, again and again and again. There is no arrival at "Okay, now I'm mindful—check!" (and the same will go for each of the other processes we will discuss in later chapters). Mindfulness is not a goal but a quality of being and doing (so, by definition, mindfulness can be a value—more on values in chapter 5).

Bring It On: Pay Attention on Purpose

Before we move on, let's pause for a simple mindfulness exercise (no cushion required!). Read the steps all the way through, then begin your practice, taking your time—about three and half minutes is all you'll need. For some of these steps, you may wish to close your eyes to more fully make contact with your experience. You can also access an audio recording of this exercise at http://www.newharbinger.com/34413 (trust me, it's easier to stay in the present moment when a voice is guiding you through it!).

1. Wherever you are right now, choose one thing you can see and look at it. Really pay attention to the details, absorbing the size, shape, color(s), texture, shading,

position. And breathe. Now look at something different and do the same. And breathe.

2. Now shift your attention to your ears and notice what you hear: sounds that are close and those that are far; sounds that are constant and those that come and go. And breathe. Try to let go of hunting for sound. Just allow your ears to receive the acoustics without names or labels. And breathe.

3. Now turn your focus to your nose. Breathe in, slowly, and see what you smell or don't smell; maybe bring your hand or arm to your nose and inhale again, taking your time, noticing any scents.

4. Now reach your hands for something. You can hold an object, or just place your hands in your lap or on the arms of your chair. Bring awareness to your sense of touch, noticing texture, temperature, weight, or any other detail available to you. And breathe. Move your hand or fingers and notice how this experience changes. Take your time.

5. Now practice purposely and flexibly shifting your attention between your senses, lingering in some places longer than others. And breathe.

6. Notice differences between your practice and your usual experience of moving through the day with your eyes, ears, nose, and hands.

In your journal, reflect on your experience. What did you notice? How was this practice different from the way you typically interact with your sensory experiences?

If you find yourself wondering how listening to your dog snore or smelling your thumb knuckle is going to help you have a mighty life, thank your mind for looking out for you—for making sure you understand what you're doing and why, and that you are not wasting your time. Learning anything new requires practice, and as a start, these exercises will help hone your ability to pay attention to the present (when we are typically in the past or future) and to shift your attention flexibly.

As we move on, you will practice greater awareness of what is happening inside your skin as well. Coming up next, we will practice letting go of judgments. Taken together, building these acuities will allow you to take your life back from your autopilot.

It Is as It Is

Now that we've practiced a bit with purposeful present-focused attention, let's fold in that third prong: *nonjudgment*.

When I first learned about mindfulness, I decided to put my new skills to the test by trying to be purposefully present in a nonjudgmental way while riding the city bus (go big or go home, right?). At the time, I was in graduate school at Boston University, where I took the #57 bus from Allston to Kenmore Square on days when it was too cold to walk (so, most days, says the girl who fled Boston for San Diego). On the day I decided to practice mindfulness, I stood at the bus stop observing the pain in my ears and the sensation of freezing in my nostrils each time I inhaled and unfreezing as I exhaled. When the third bus passed me by (the colder it was, the fuller they got!), I noticed a feeling of desperation and an urge to cry.

Once I was finally picked up, I paid attention to the shifting tension in my quads as I tried to balance myself with nothing to hold on to. I noticed the sensation of bodies bumping into mine and the bead of sweat trickling down my temple. I smelled a mix of unidentifiable smells. I watched the trees whiz by outside.

Now, mindfully standing in the freezing cold followed by mindfully riding a hot, crowded, public bus, did not magically make these experiences pleasant and fun. But being mindful did make them less unpleasant, and here's why: paying attention to the present moment *nonjudgmentally* means making direct contact with actual, in-the-moment experience, and letting go of the troublemaker known as language (specifically, predicting, problem solving, planning, evaluating, and comparing). Said another way, mindfulness allows experiences to be as they are, rather than what the mind says they are.

The pre-mindful me suffered the #57 bus as a result of my Inner Judge and her never-ending critical narration of the experience: "I hate the cold, this is awful, being too short to reach the handles is the worst, it's a billion degrees in here, stupid winter, stupid bus, stupid city" (my Inner Judge can be a tad childish). The mindful me simply observed her experience as it arose, however it happened to be, in that one moment, and in the next, and the next.

To be clear, the *purpose* of mindfulness is *not* to change an experience from extremely unpleasant to less unpleasant: that just happens to be a nice by-product. Cultivating mindfulness means greater awareness of internal experiences in the absence of judgment (or letting go of judgments each time they arise), which threatens to steer us away from living our best lives.

Greater awareness creates space between detonator (internal experiences) and bomb (impulsive reactions). In that space, bombs can be deactivated through acceptance, defusion, contact with values, and deliberate choice in service of those values (more on these specific ACT processes in later chapters). A mind*less* angry bus lady (detonator) may be at risk for punching the next passenger who bumps into her (bomb); a mind*ful* passenger's experience just is as it is. Bomb neutralized.

Bring It On: Dust in the Wind

Before we move on, let's pause to practice mindfulness with a specific focus on noticing and letting go of judgments. For this practice, you will need access to music. Ideally, you will download or stream "Dust in the Wind" by Kansas (this should be freely available on

YouTube as long as you have access to the Internet). If you can't locate this song, you can use any song and still follow the remaining instructions.

Find a space where you will be uninterrupted for the duration of the song (three and a half minutes). Read this once through before you begin. Once you play the song, close your eyes if you are willing.

1. Allow your attention to rest on one specific element within the music, perhaps just the guitar at first, lingering for a bit.

2. Then shift your attention to something else, perhaps the lead singer's voice or the harmony when the two sing together, or the overall melody.

3. Flexibly shift your attention, observing the diverse features of the piece.

4. As you shift your attention, also observe your reactions.

5. Notice any physical or emotional feelings that arise, and how these transform as verse turns to refrain and refrain shifts to bridge.

6. Importantly, pay particular attention to judgments, positive or negative ("I love this song," "I hate this song," "the harmonizing is like nails on a chalkboard," and so forth), and associations (past memories or other connections your mind makes to the lyrics or other elements of the song; "You're my boy, Blue!").

7. For three and a half minutes, move your attention around your internal and sensory experiences, gently bringing your attention back any time you find it has strayed elsewhere.

8. Notice each time a judgment arises, then imagine it blowing in the wind, much like dust would blow in the wind, lightly dancing, rarely seen landing.

You're not trying to blow the judgment away to get rid of it; you are merely acting as an observer of your judgments, catching sight of them like you might catch sight of dust in the wind. When we catch sight of dust, we don't try to grab it, push it away, or control it; if we did, it would just keep blowing out of our reach. Instead, we notice and move on.

Repeat this practice throughout your week using assorted sensory stimuli, such as video, food, drink, visual art, or other music. Choose something you are likely to form a judgment about (positive or negative), so that you can practice observing the features of your sensory and emotional experience, while simultaneously catching judgments as they arise. As you notice judgments, practice letting them go like dust in the wind. This will allow you to practice acceptance (the topic of the next chapter) as well. Feel free to journal about your experience, though ongoing physical practice will be the most potent ingredient for strengthening your mindfulness muscles.

THE ZONE

If mindfulness is purposeful, nonjudgmental, present-focused awareness, we might think of mind*less*ness as wavering, evaluative, past- or future-focused awareness. So what about "being in the zone" or experiencing a sense of "flow" (Nakamura and Csikszentmihalyi 2009)? This intensely immersive, hyper-focused state of attention is often reported by competitive athletes, artists, writers, and musicians. Time and all other distractions evaporate, replaced by a keen sense of clarity, heightened productivity, and increased creative output. Is this mindfulness? It certainly seems to check the boxes.

A critical element of mindfulness, however, is *flexible*, or interactive, attention. This means we *choose* what to attend to and for how long, and then choose again, shifting attention as needed, in the service of psychological flexibility.

If you have kids, you have probably observed them in the zone as they play their favorite video games. What happens when you call their names, trying to get their attention? I typically have to address mine at least three times, getting progressively louder with each repetition. Being in the zone means being completely sucked in. There is sustained hyper-attention to one aspect of the present experience, but it lacks flexibility; there is no interaction. This isn't necessarily problematic if being "sucked in" has no cost, and what you are sucked into matters to you. But it becomes a concern when it functions as experiential avoidance or causes other important areas of your life to be neglected. Being sucked in may or may not be psychologically flexible.

Bring It On: Beware the Danger Zone

Before we move on, let's investigate you in the zone. Bring to mind an experience when you felt like you were hyper-focused, a moment when you were so engrossed in some activity that you lost track of time and were immune to distraction. In your journal, respond to the following prompts:

* What were you doing and what characterized the situation as a zone state?

* In what ways were you psychologically flexible or inflexible? As a reminder, psychological flexibility means awareness of and openness to all internal experiences coupled with a deliberate choice to engage in ways that personally matter to you. Inflexibility is characterized by actions dictated by thoughts or feelings in the absence of guiding values. For example, an inflexible zone might include a time when you were sucked into social media, causing you to miss out on interacting with your partner or kids. A flexible zone might include a time when you were creating, sailing, or having sex—100 percent in

that moment and only in that moment, in an area of life that matters to you, and without cost.

✳ How might more purposeful, interactive, present-focused attention help you identify a flexible zone versus a danger zone? How might it pull you out of a danger zone or turn a less flexible zone into a more flexible zone?

THE TAKEAWAY

Mindfulness—paying attention to the present, on purpose, and non-judgmentally—provides the scaffolding for everything in this book. We can't change our response to that of which we are not aware. To become more psychologically flexible—opening to and allowing our internal and sensory experiences as they are, rather than what the mind says they are, and choosing to do what matters—we must learn to cultivate mindfulness. Nonjudgmental attention to the present does not equate to an absence of judging, past-focused, or future-focused thoughts, nor does it mean pushing those thoughts away as they arise. Importantly, it simply means awareness of those thoughts as a step toward consciously chosen responding.

Mindfulness is the key to unlocking the space between detonator and bomb, where we can slow down, observe, and experience the moment fully and without defense. This disables our autopilot, deactivates our bomb, and allows us to discover and experience life, as it is, rather than what the mind says it is.

Chapter 4

Wielding the Weapon of Willingness

You can never leave footprints that last if you are always walking on tiptoe.

—Leymah Gbowee

Now that you understand the importance of shedding the shackles of avoidance and honing the powers of presence, let's talk about what to do instead of avoiding when we become aware of our internal discomfort. We've established that (1) avoidance only "works" temporarily and often makes things worse in the long run, and (2) avoidance often interferes with the things that matter most (family, friends, school, work, adventure, fun, romance). So what's the alternative to the Big A (Avoidance)? Answer: the other, *bigger* A: *Acceptance*.

"Acceptance" simply refers to the process of opening up and allowing whatever emotions, sensations, or urges show up, to just be, without doing anything to control or resist them (Hayes, Strosahl, and Wilson 1999). Your anxiety, worry, and uncertainty are here, so you choose to let them be here. You wield the weapon of *willingness*.

This might be when you notice Ms. Resistance chiming in: "What?! No way! Why on earth would I do that?!" The answer? See numbers 1 and 2 in the paragraph above (or go back and engage with any of the experiential practices in chapter 2). Also, because many scientific studies have demonstrated the advantages of acceptance over experiential avoidance. I want to be clear: acceptance does *not* mean liking or wanting anxiety. That would make you a masochist, in which case you would need to read an entirely different book! It simply means making space for what is already here anyway.

SENSATIONAL STUDIES

If you're a nerd like me, check this out: multiple research studies have demonstrated the advantages of practicing acceptance of anxiety as an alternative to avoidance. In one study, participants who had been diagnosed with an anxiety disorder were exposed to emotionally distressing movie clips and taught to respond to their emotions by either accepting their experience or trying to suppress it. Those who practiced acceptance experienced reduced fight-or-flight reactions and faster recovery from emotional distress compared with those who practiced control strategies (Campbell-Sills et al. 2006).

When a group of individuals diagnosed with panic disorder participated in a task to deliberately bring on panic sensations, those who were taught acceptance reported lower levels of anxiety and a greater willingness to repeat the task compared to those who were taught to suppress the panic. Interestingly, this was true despite both groups reporting equal physiological sensations (Levitt et al. 2004).

Similar results have been found in studies of food cravings (Hooper et al. 2012), physical pain (Masedo and Esteve 2007), and mood disorders as well (Liverant et al. 2008).

THE UNWILLINGNESS PARADOX

If you're still not feeling it, try looking at it this way: imagine I have you in a little booth suspended above a barracuda tank. I tell you, "Whatever you do, just don't get anxious and you will be fine.

Unfortunately, if you *do* get anxious, the floor of the booth will open, dropping you into the barracuda tank. But, no worries, just don't get anxious and you will be totally fine!"

What do you think is going to happen? Right—you're anxious… and fish food. Is it because you just didn't try hard enough to control your anxiety? Was the incentive not quite high enough? Of course not—our most primitive instinct is to survive. So why did you get anxious and end up swimming with the fishes? Because when you are *unwilling* to experience anxiety, *you are anxious about anxiety,* so you are anxious (Hayes, Strosahl, and Wilson 1999).

See the trap? Your relationship to anxiety becomes one in which anxiety is evaluated as bad, dangerous, and deadly. So, of course, you are anxious about having anxiety. Unwilling to have it, you've got it. How often do you hear on *Good Morning America* or in the *Huffington Post* "Stress is bad for you! Stress will kill you! You shouldn't get stressed!" What happens? You stress about having stress, so you're stressed! Unwilling to have it, you've got it.

This might be where that sneaky experiential avoidance creeps in and says, "Ooh, so if I'm *unwilling* to have it, I've got it, which means if I *am* willing to have it, it will go away?" Sorry, nope, doesn't work that way. If you're unwilling to have it, you've got it. If you're willing to have it, anxiety will do what anxiety does—ebb and flow, rise and fall, come and go.

Bring It On: Yes Battles No

Before we move on, let's pause to experientially connect to the difference between struggling to avoid internal experiences versus opening and allowing them to be as they are (Stoddard and Afari 2014). To start, shift your attention to your body.

1. Notice your feet on the floor or in your shoes. Notice the way the furniture or floor supports your body.

2. Now zero in on the sensations of your back against the chair, floor, or whatever surface you are resting on.

3. Each time you notice a sensation—touch, contact, pressure, pain, itch—do your best to avoid experiencing the sensations you notice.

4. For the next two minutes, whenever you notice the sensation of your back against the chair, say no to it: do whatever it takes to suppress, stop, restrict, control, distract from, or avoid experiencing the sensation of your back against the surface it is resting against. Close your eyes for the two minutes, so you can really focus on pushing the sensations away.

5. Once the first two minutes are up, continue to keep your focus on the sensations in your back. But for the next two minutes, shift your *response* to those sensations.

6. For the next two minutes, accept those sensations.

7. Say yes to those sensations: be willing to feel the sensations, simply as sensations, whatever they may be.

8. Observe the sensations, open up to them, expand around them, allow whatever shows up to just be.

9. Let go of resistance.

10. In your journal, reflect on your experience. What did you notice? Were you successful at avoiding the sensations in your back? How did your experience differ when you said yes versus no?

Often, people report no real change in sensations, but they do feel a notable decrease in tension, distress, and effort when practicing willingness instead of struggling to avoid. This week, practice shifting between purposely resisting a difficult internal experience (emotion, sensation, urge), then practicing willingness toward that same experience. Notice the differences, and reflect on this in your journal as you go.

ACCEPTANCE IN ACTION

Here's another counterintuitive idea. The acceptance we've been talking about is not a feeling. It's an action. You can act willingly even when you don't feel willing (Hayes and Smith 2005). The feeling of willingness may come and go, like day and night. Acting willingly is about establishing a different response when anxiety shows up. It's not something we *try* to do, it's something we do. In the wise words of Jedi Master Yoda, "Do or do not, there is no try."

During the "Yes Battles No" exercise, you may not have felt willing, especially if you happen to suffer from back pain. And yet, you were able to *choose a new response* (not to try to choose, but to choose) as you noticed the sensations in your back, whether you *felt* willing or not. In fact, the ancient root of the word *willing* means "to choose" (Hayes and Smith 2005)—we don't choose how we feel, we choose what we do and how we do it.

You've probably had the experience of not feeling willing if you've ever shared a flight with a crying baby. You board a plane and discover you have the whole row to yourself. You think, *Perfect! I can stretch out and really get some sleep* (Stoddard and Afari 2014). Then, just before the cabin door is closed, a young couple comes onboard with a screaming infant. You think to yourself, *The poor people who have to sit next to them all night,* just as the couple arrives at your row. You shuffle your stuff to make room for them, but in your head you're screaming, *Noooooo!*

The parents try everything to soothe the baby. They try the bottle, and that just makes him scream louder. They try his favorite toy, but he keeps screaming. What are your options here? You can spend the next eight hours giving them dirty looks, scoffing at their failed attempts to quiet their child, and letting them know that this kind of behavior is absolutely unacceptable on a plane. Alternatively, you could join them in trying to quiet the child: playing peekaboo, giving the child your phone to fiddle with—anything to quiet the kid down (which ends up hijacking your entire flying experience, so to speak).

Or, whether or not you *feel* willing, you could choose to do what you would usually do on a flight, all the while taking in the sounds of that child as they are and recognizing that the child is doing what children do. This is not wanting or liking the sounds the child is making, but also not needing the sounds not to be there. And all the while, you're also noticing that no matter how long the child cries, he won't cry forever, and that wanting him to quiet down will never be what's needed for him to do so.

Acceptance Is All In

Acceptance is also an all-in action—it is not conditional. In other words, true acceptance does not mean allowing the anxiety to a point and then shifting back to avoidance every time a certain unwanted level of discomfort is reached (Hayes and Smith 2005). It's like swinging high on a swing and jumping off. You either jump or you don't. You can't jump halfway. You might say, "Yes, but I can choose to swing high or low." Absolutely. You can take baby steps in your actions. But each and every one will require all-in willingness. If the swing is low, you either jump or you don't. If the swing is high, you jump or you don't.

If you're anxious about driving, practicing acceptance doesn't mean you must immediately start driving alone at night in the rain on an eight-lane freeway in the fast lane. It can mean driving in a parking lot with someone you trust, as long as you are 100 percent willing while you are engaged in that chosen action.

Whatever size step you choose is just right—the only requirement for that step to improve your psychological flexibility (which is always our overarching goal) is that the choice is based on something that matters to you, and that you engage in it with 100 percent willingness.

Bring It On: Mindful Willingness

Before we move on, let's pause for a practice that can help you strengthen your all-in acceptance muscles. To prepare for this exercise, sit comfortably in a chair and read through the script in its entirety before you begin. (Alternatively, you can access the guided audio at http://www.newharbinger.com/34413, which I highly recommend.) Throughout the exercise, and when you use it going forward, remember, it is not intended to be a relaxation exercise. You may very well feel more relaxed, and that is a nice bonus. However, its purpose is acceptance of what is, not pushing away what you'd rather not experience.

To begin, consider your anxiety and how you experience it. How do you know when you're anxious? Where do you feel it in your body? When this becomes clear, close your eyes and allow your attention to settle on your breath.

1. Observe the air as it enters and exits your body, noticing the sensations of the air in your nostrils and on your upper lip.

2. Notice the sound of your breath or the lack of sound.

3. Notice the movement of your breath, the gentle rise and fall of your chest or belly. Notice how the body physically expands with every inhale.

4. Now, as you breathe, allow every inhale to be a vehicle to expand the places where you experience anxiety.

5. As you exhale, let go of resistance.

6. Inhale, open to anxiety. Exhale, surrender the battle.

7. Inhale, allow discomfort. Exhale, drop the struggle.

8. As you breathe, you might say things to yourself like, *Okay... This is here now... I have space for this... There is nothing that needs to be done here... Let go.*

9. You might let your shoulders drop, your teeth separate, your face smooth, your belly let go (we sometimes hold resistance in our bodies).

10. Inhale, expand to make space, and allow what you feel to just be as it is. Exhale, let go of resistance.

11. Inhale willingness. Exhale avoidance.

Your breath is always with you and can provide a powerful means for channeling willingness.

Acceptance Is Not

Hopefully it's pretty clear that when we talk about acceptance and willingess, we are specifically talking about acceptance of *internal experiences*. We are not talking about acceptance of situations. For example, we are not talking about acceptance of sexist behavior or abuse; we are talking about acceptance of the hurt, anger, and sadness that arise when we are mistreated, especially insofar as acceptance expands our options for freely choosing what to do and how to do it.

In other words, we can make space for the hurt *and* still continue to have a voice and take up space, rather than shrinking back to avoid the pain. We can also find strength in practicing self-acceptance.

Bring It On: Self-Acceptance

For the following imagery exercise, we are going to take a trip into your childhood—to around the age of six, seven, or eight years old, to a time or specific experience or memory when you remember feeling sad, lonely, inadequate, unlovable, or unseen (Walser and Westrup 2007).

Read through each of the following paragraphs, one at a time, pausing in between each one to close your eyes and make full contact with the imagery. (Alternatively, you can access the guided audio at http://www.newharbinger.com/34413, which beats interrupting your practice to read.) Take the perspective of your six-, seven-, or eight-year-old self, seeing things through her eyes.

1. Picture what you looked like at that young age—your little-girl haircut, your outfit, your shoes, your small

hands and little feet. Close your eyes, making contact with the image until it crystallizes.

2. Now imagine that you're going back to your childhood home. Picture the outside of your home, as if you are little you, standing on the sidewalk, looking at the details of the outside of the place you called home. Notice how, because of your small height, you have to sort of look up to take in the whole thing. Close your eyes, allowing yourself to really see it.

3. Now walk up to your front door. Notice how it takes more steps as a little girl, because your legs are so much shorter. If there are steps to the front door, perhaps you have to reach up to hold the railing, taking the steps as small people do. Close your eyes, taking it all in, and breathe.

4. When you get to the door, reach up, open the door, and walk inside. Look all around, picturing the details there—the paint or wallpaper on the walls, the carpet or other flooring, the furniture and decor. Notice whether you find a familiar smell or sound there. Close your eyes and allow yourself to emerge in your childhood home.

5. Now go to the room where you would most likely find your mother or mother figure. Notice the details of what you see as you walk there, and how your eye line is a lot lower than it would be today. When you reach your mother (figure), watch her for a few moments (she doesn't see you yet). Notice how she looks, what she's wearing, how her hair is styled, what she is doing. Close your eyes and connect. Notice how you feel.

6. Walk up to your mother (figure) and get her attention—call her name or give a little tug on her clothes—and get her to look down at you, into your eyes. Notice the

expression on her face. Close your eyes, meeting hers, and breathe.

7. Now, from that early place of sadness, loneliness, or feeling inadequate, unlovable, or unseen, ask your mother (figure) for whatever it is you might need. Close your eyes, pause, see if she is able to provide it.

8. Now, softly disconnecting from your mother (figure), turn and go to where you would find your father or father figure. Notice the details of what you see as you walk there. When you reach your father (figure), watch him for a few moments (he doesn't see you yet). Notice how he looks, what he's wearing, how his hands or hair appear, what he is doing. Close your eyes and contact the details. Notice how you feel.

9. Walk up to your father (figure) and get his attention— say his name or give a little tap, tap, tap on his body— and get him to look down at you, into your eyes. Notice the expression on his face. Close your eyes, meeting his, and breathe.

10. Now, from that early place of sadness, loneliness, or feeling inadequate, unlovable, or unseen, ask your father (figure) for whatever it is you might need. Close your eyes, pause, see if he is able to provide it.

11. Now softly disconnect from your father (figure) and walk back to the front door, noticing the details of what you see, smell, and hear as you go. Let yourself out, closing the door softly behind you, returning to the front of your home. Close your eyes, feel the sun on your face or the wind on your skin, and breathe.

12. Begin to walk away from your home. In the distance, notice a grownup walking toward you. As the figure

approaches, you recognize her—she is you, today. Walk until little you and big you are standing face to face. Look up at that big you, seeing your adult face through the eyes of your younger self. Close your eyes, you looking at you.

13. Now, from that early place of sadness, loneliness, or feeling inadequate, unlovable, or unseen, have little you ask big you for whatever it is that you need. Close your eyes, breathe, and give your small self what she needs, lingering as long as you need.

14. Now softly disconnect and come back to the present, the adult you back behind your adult eyes, seeing everything as it is right now.

15. And now imagine that little six-, seven-, or eight-year-old you has walked into the room and is walking toward you right now. She is here, now, standing right in front of you—the same little girl haircut, outfit, small hands—and she is tugging on your sleeve, asking for your attention. Get on her level, cup her sweet face in your hands, give her your attention.

16. Look into her small face, her longing eyes, and see what it is that this small person needs. See if you can give her what she needs, fully and without defense. If you notice resistance, see if you can let it go and give her what she needs. Close your eyes, notice how you feel, taking your time, sitting with it.

17. Now imagine that little you climbs up onto your lap. As you hold her and breathe with her, you begin to merge into one. Your small self becomes part of your big self, your big self accepts the child self as part of her, as part of you. Close your eyes, allowing the warmth of self-acceptance and love to spread through you.

Reflect on your experience. This exercise isn't intended to heal old wounds or take away pain. Its imagery is meant to provide a pathway to embody self-acceptance through alternating perspectives.

WATERFALLS OF WILLINGNESS

To embody acceptance, you might think of yourself as water (Hayes and Ciarrochi 2015). Water adapts. If it is unobstructed, it simply flows. If it meets an object, like a pier in the ocean, it doesn't stop, nor does it need the object to be removed; it simply flows around the pylons, continuing on its journey to shore. Water makes room for what is inside of it. If a body is added to a bathtub, the water rises to share the space.

An ice cube can be made from water then placed in a glass of water; they are different in appearance, texture, and temperature, and while they are fundamentally made of the same stuff, they are also separate from one another. Water can be still and reflective, like a lake on a summer morning. Water can flow playfully and musically, like a bubbling brook. And water can move fast and aggressively, like a white-water river rapid.

Like water, you can adapt and flow around obstacles toward what matters. Like water, you can share space for what comes in. Like water, your thoughts, emotions, sensations, and urges come from you, and while they look and feel different, they are made of similar stuff. And yet they are also separate from you. Like water, you are sometimes still, sometimes playful, and sometimes crashing mightily. In this way, you can *choose* how and where to direct your energy, based on what the situation and your values demand.

That is not to say that acceptance means we ought to feel anxiety or other pain for pain's sake—there is no victory to sitting in pain for the heck of it. Acceptance is allowing the anxiety; because not doing so, fighting it, is getting in the way of the stuff that really matters.

Remember when I said in chapter 2 that avoidance is only problematic when it has a cost? That's where the willingness comes in. If getting a massage makes you feel calmer, there's nothing wrong with that! Of course, if you're so unwilling to feel your anxiety that you've taken out a second mortgage to pay for your twice-daily massages and you have no time to be with friends or family, now there's a cost—and willingness will need to take the place of Franchesca's famous fingers if you truly want to be mighty.

Metaphorically, it's like choosing to travel to visit someone you love. The trip is typically long and expensive. But there is no rule saying the hard way is the best way. If you can teleport for free, go for it! However, if you're not living on the Starship *Enterprise* with Scotty, can you be *willing* to do the harder thing—spend the money, or take the overnight flight with two connections—if this is the only way to be with the person you care about?

Bring It On: Women Who Kick But

If you are going to choose willingness in your quest to be mighty, try kicking some serious but. No, that is not a typo. I'm talking "but," not "butt" (although that can be mighty too). In your journal, fill in the following sentence:

I really want to _____ [action I long to engage in], *but* _____ [feeling I don't want to have that gets in my way].

This might look something like:

I really want to start dating, but I'm afraid of being rejected.

I really want to apply for the promotion, but I'm uncertain whether I'm qualified.

I've always dreamed of going back to school, but I'm worried everyone will think I'm too old or I won't have what it takes.

Write down all of your personal examples that come to mind.

Next, strap on your but-kicking shoes and boot those buts right out of your sentences, replacing each one with the word "and" (Hayes and Smith 2005). I want to date, *and* I fear rejection; I want to go for the promotion, *and* I'm not sure I'm qualified; I want to return to school *and* I'm worried about it.

What do you notice? Where does your *but* lead you? The answer: down the path of avoidance (**A**nxiety x **S**truggle = **S**uffering; the acronym is no coincidence!). Whereas your *and* epitomizes willingness and opens up the path to psychological flexibility and a mighty life.

THE TAKEAWAY

Acceptance is the opposite of experiential avoidance. If experiential avoidance is an unwillingness to feel discomfort and active efforts to control it, acceptance is an active choice to turn toward discomfort—not for the sake of white-knuckling through it, nor in the service of giving up or giving in, but as a way to increase behavioral options so that you can more flexibly and freely respond to the present moment in ways that move you toward a mighty life. When difficult internal experiences trigger your detonator, mindfulness unlocks the space between detonator and bomb, and *willingness* is one mighty tool to help deactivate the explosive device.

Acceptance creates a context for greater engagement in rich and meaningful life experiences, many of which are only available to us when we are willing to feel all the feels.

Chapter 5

Declaring Victory
Through Values

You are the one that possesses the keys to your being.

—Diane von Furstenberg

Hopefully, you've been getting some practice flexing your mighty mindfulness and acceptance muscles. And, if you have, you've no doubt noticed how tough it can be! In a tug-of-war competition, the pull of experiential avoidance (in its many forms) could give the pull of gravity a run for its money! As you continue to read and learn, there will likely be more than a few occasions when you experience frustration and feel like you're not "getting it" or not "doing it right."

You may not believe this, but I still feel this way sometimes, and I've been practicing ACT for more than fifteen years. I don't share this to discourage you ("You mean I still won't get it after fifteen years?! What's the point?!") but to take the opportunity to remind you of something very important: *there are no arrivals.*

The process of building psychological flexibility is one that is ongoing. Being open (acceptance) and aware (mindfulness) are positions we must choose to return to again and again and again. And we will fail. A lot. And each time we notice an unworkable choice or pattern of choices, we can choose to come back to willingness and values—doing what matters, the Me you want to be—in the very next moment. In this chapter, we will unpack what values mean to you.

You will also likely have moments when you "forget" why you're replacing avoidance with acceptance. Avoidance brings relief, after all, and acceptance, in the service of doing what matters, can be painful. When this forgetting occurs, and the Inner Rebel shows up asking, "Why am I making stupid space for this stupid anxiety again?" (my Inner Rebel is as childish as my Inner Judge) you need only one thing to remind you: your experience.

You don't need fancy experts to answer the question why; you *are* the fancy expert. You're the expert who can plainly see that when you look to your stuck places, Her Majesty, Avoidance, is usually ruling the queendom, manipulating you with her tempting promises of relief while holding you hostage in the Tiny Tower of the Comfort Zone. So when that childish rebel shows up kicking and screaming ("But I don't wanna feel the feelings!"), remind her of the might of mindfulness, hand her the weapon of willingness, and send her off to dethrone that evil Avoidance queen.

Of course, being mighty isn't just about cultivating mindfulness and brandishing our willingness weapons. It's also about charging into the lives we truly desire. Sometimes "what I truly desire" may seem a bit murky.

In your mind, complete the following statements quickly and spontaneously: "I want to be _____. I want my life to be _____." If you're like most, your answer pair was probably some version of "happy/less stressful" (less anxious/easier, and so on). Of course you want those things! But you also now understand that we don't get to choose how we feel. If the criteria for a life well lived rest on controlling our feelings, we will never have the lives we want. So we need new criteria. What I'm talking about here are values: the qualities of being and doing that we care most deeply about. The Me you want to be.

Bring It On: Sweetness

Before we move on, let's take a minute to make contact with an experience that will allow what you care about to begin to emerge. We've talked a lot about the hurt places; now I'd like to switch gears. I'd like for you to think about a moment in your life when you experienced sweetness—an experience you had when maybe you let go of the struggle with your thoughts and feelings, even if just for a few moments (Wilson and DuFrene 2009). It doesn't have to be the biggest or most monumental thing that's happened—or it could be. Just pick any specific moment—big or small, recent or long past—when you felt really present, engaged, or alive.

Here's a personal example so you might get a sense of what I mean:

I parked my car in the driveway after a long day of work. As I approached the front door, I was aware of how heavy my shoulder bag felt and the sluggishness in my step. I opened the door and took two steps inside; the long hallway stretched out in front of me. Suddenly, I heard two little (yet big) voices exclaim, "Moooommmmm-mmmmmyyyyyyyyyy!!!!!!!" followed by two miniature human bodies sprinting toward me, radiating expressions of pure excitement and joy, plus two squat French Bulldog bodies lumbering behind, snorting like little piggies. I was enveloped in hugs and kisses, both human and canine, all of us brimming with pure love. In that moment, I thought, *My sweet, sweet babies.* It was a thirty-second moment that was completely perfect and sweet.

Now choose a sweet moment of your own. It doesn't have to be like mine. It could be visiting with your grandmother, watching a sunset, or crossing a finish line—anything whatsoever.

You might find yourself snagged in mental gymnastics, trying to choose exactly the right thing. See if you can notice that and let it go, just allowing any moment of sweetness to bubble to the surface (the good news is, you can return to this exercise again if you want to visit more sweet moments!). Whichever you choose, just make sure it's a specific memory, and revisit that moment. As you read the following paragraph, the details will begin to fill in. Consider reading it all the way through once, then closing your eyes to encounter this sweet experience in full Technicolor. (You can also access a recording of this exercise at http://www.newharbinger.com/34413.)

As you revisit your moment of sweetness, look around in your mind's eye and notice all the details that were present, kind of like looking at a color photograph that fully captures everything about that perfect, sweet moment. Notice the details of your surroundings—where you are, what you're doing, and who you're with. Notice the expression on your face and the look in your eyes. Allow your awareness to pour itself into the you in that picture at that moment. Emerge in that space and:

* Let yourself see what you see there.

* Let yourself hear the sounds of your surroundings.

* Notice what you smell.

* Notice the sensations that you feel on your skin in that place. If you're outdoors, perhaps you feel the heat of the sun or the cold of the wind on your skin. If you're with someone, you might feel the warmth of that person's body against yours.

Breathe that moment in, allowing each breath to fill you with its sweetness. Let every ounce of you feel what it is to be in that moment. Let the sweetness satiate and nourish your soul.

Now, using your journal, give expression to that sweet moment, jotting down the details you noticed. Reflecting back, write about what your experience might tell you about some of the things that matter to you. You might notice themes of connection—with people, animals, or nature. You might notice qualities of openness, engagement, playfulness, adventure, vulnerability, or wonder. Explore the meaning or importance of where you were, who you were with, what you were doing, and how you were doing it.

Also reflect on whether your sweet moment might even contain some pain just on the other side of it (such as the fear of loss that comes with allowing yourself to love deeply) and your choice to show up and engage anyway. Notice whether your experience connects with the idea that we hurt when we care. And yet, maybe the juice is worth the squeeze.

Observe and reflect on how present you were during your moment of sweetness—if you hadn't been present, you could not have experienced (nor remembered) that sweetness. You would have missed the moment. And the moments matter.

In many cultures, we are led to believe that life is all about the big stuff: graduations, weddings, babies, turning thirty or forty or fifty. But even in a long life of eighty or ninety years, we can probably count on two hands the number of these we get. So what is the rest of our existence? Small moments weaved together. If we're not showing up, participating fully and without defense, especially for the sweet ones (or the ones when we experience wonder or awe, or feel more alive or inspired), no matter how small, how mighty a life can we possibly have?

In previous chapters, you have read phrases like "doing what matters," living a "full and meaningful life," "workable behavior," "what you care most deeply about," and "the Me you want to be." All of these have been pointing to *values* in ACT. Look at the sweet moment you chose for the exercise you just completed. You chose it for a reason, and it highlights where you care. In my personal example, family, love, connection, affection, being present, and coming home jump right off the page. What jumps off yours? Your answer is our surface scratcher for unpacking your most deeply held personal values.

IN THIS ONE MOMENT

Simply put, values are the qualities of being and doing that represent the person you most deeply desire to be—the Me you want to be. They are *what* we choose to do (or not do) and *how* we choose to do it. When we consistently choose to act in accordance with our values, life expands to include greater meaning, vibrancy, and fulfillment. Opportunities to make values-driven choices occur in thousands of small and subtle ways every day.

This hit me like a ton of bricks one day when I was speeding, er driving, down the freeway in San Diego, California. At that time, I drove a Mini Cooper convertible. I loved this car; it was fast and fun. And red. Having grown up in the Boston area, my driving style was a little, shall we say, aggressive? I was cruising along in the left lane when my unencumbered journey was suddenly impeded by a slow driver who apparently never got the memo that left lanes are reserved for the speedy. My Inner Bully showed up. I thought, possibly audibly, *Come on, man, move over! This is the fast lane, ya jerk!* My body got tense, I felt immensely irritated, and my autopilot took over the controls. I got right up on his bumper and flashed my lights, feeling righteous and thinking, *I'll show him. Jerk.* (My Inner Bully is the real jerk.)

But in the next beat, I thought, *Really? Is this what you want to be about in your life? Trying to intimidate strangers into driving faster or changing lanes so you can get somewhere thirty seconds faster?* And the answer was no. I wanted (and still want) to be someone who chooses kindness, understanding, and consideration as I navigate my life (and my car). So I backed off. *Values are qualities of being and doing* (kindness, understanding, and consideration)—*they are what we choose to do, or not do* (tailgate or drive at a safe distance), *and how we choose to do it* (rudely or respectfully). Values are the Me you want to be.

I didn't know the pokey driver, nor would I ever meet him. It was simply about choosing the type of human—the Me—I wanted to be *in that one moment.* Maybe it's no coincidence that "me" sits inside "moment." Do you see it? moMEnt. When my Inner Bully showed up and snatched away the wheel, connecting to my values gave me the power to reclaim the drive. These seemingly small or insignificant points in time matter. In fact, maybe they are not small at all. Maybe they add up—to a life more mighty.

Bring It On: The Me I Choose to Be

Bring to mind a recent seemingly small or insignificant moment when you felt less than proud of your comportment. Maybe you sent a passive-aggressive text or snapped at someone you care about; maybe you saw someone you recognized and pretended not to see him or her; maybe you told a fib. Now describe the situation by responding to the following in your journal:

* What thoughts and feelings did the situation trigger in you?

* What did you do or not do?

* What did that choice get you (how did you immediately feel)? Notice how even a small thing has its purpose—*it works or you wouldn't do it*. (Tailgating and flashing my lights made me feel powerful in a situation I couldn't control.)

* Was the choice in line with the Me you truly wish to be? If that Me could hit rewind and have a do-over, what would she do differently and why?

ACTIONS AND QUALITIES OF ACTIONS

Part of the values equation is in choosing what we do or don't do. Let's look at an example. Friendship is very important to Alex. So she chooses to reach out to her friends and invite them for a girls' night out. She feels worried that they will all decline, or that they will think it's weird she is initiating plans when that's not typical of her. But she chooses to do it anyway, because being with her friends really matters to her. Her chosen actions—organizing and attending girls' night out—are values consistent.

When Alex goes to dinner with her gal pals, she talks a lot about the weather and traffic; she doesn't think she has anything interesting to contribute. When she talks about her kids and her relationship, she plasters on a smile and overemphasizes the good stuff ("Johnny got all A's on his report card!" "Spouse got me a great birthday gift!") and leaves out the really hard stuff ("Johnny has no friends and comes home crying every day. I have no idea how to help him and it breaks my heart." "Spouse and I haven't had sex in eight months. I feel so distant and I'm not sure how to fix it."). Alex is afraid of being judged. She assumes her friends can't possibly relate, because, unlike her, they all have their acts together.

Alex's chosen actions of organizing and attending girls' night out land solidly in the first half of the values box. But, it turns out, the qualities she embodied—superficial, disingenuous, and avoidant—while interacting with her friends were not at all those that represent the Me she wants to be. More than anything, Alex deeply desires to be open and real, especially with the people she cares about. Those *qualities* of her actions are the other half of the values equation.

Other examples of qualities might include courageous, playful, kind, curious, creative, honest, independent, reliable, competent, respectful (to self or others), or compassionate. For a more comprehensive list of example qualities, visit http://www.newharbinger.com/34413 and refer to The Me I Want to Be info sheet. You can refer to this as we continue to flesh out your personal values.

Bring It On: Fierce Favorites

To further unpack your values, bring to mind a favorite person or character whom you admire or who inspires you, someone who has made choices and possesses qualities that matter to you (Stoddard and Afari 2014). This can be someone you know personally—a friend, colleague, or teacher, perhaps—or it can be someone you only know of, such as a public figure or fictional character.

Now think about what you admire most in this person—not what the person has accumulated or achieved but her or his chosen actions and personal qualities or character. Write it down in your journal. It's okay if you don't know (or even like) everything about this person. Just speak to whichever actions and qualities earn this person fierce favorite status in your eyes. You can consider more than one favorite; write about that person's actions and qualities as well.

Look over your entry and consider how your fierce favorite might inspire your own personal values. What qualities does she or he possess that you feel are important for you to embody as well? For example, you may notice she or he is bold, ambitious, kind, or creative. Perhaps she or he has chosen to persevere through adversity or rejection despite fear or self-doubt.

I had one client who chose Ellen DeGeneres as her fierce favorite because Ellen bravely came out about her sexuality, in service of being her authentic self, despite knowing she would likely face a difficult professional (and perhaps personal) backlash. She advocates for compassion and animal rights, and she is generous, playful, and funny.

My fierce favorite is Oprah because she persevered through poverty, abuse, sexism, and racism, all while struggling with her weight and body image (a deep pain I relate to), but never letting any of it stop her from having a voice, being her authentic self, and making a difference—and she uses her power for good.

How are you like and unlike your favorite? In this one moment, and the next, how might you embody the characteristics of your fierce favorite that feel deeply important to the Me you want to be?

PERSONAL AND FREELY CHOSEN

As you delve further into your values, check to ensure that they are, indeed, *your values*. What I mean is, values are deeply personal and consciously chosen, *by us and only us*; not by our parents, peers, society, culture, or religion. Of course, some of our values will undoubtedly align with those of our parents, peers, or pastors, but the key is *free choice*.

Consider some of the messages you have received throughout your life about the way you are "supposed to" be. As Republicans, my parents' values centered around self-sufficiency; while they valued generosity inside their own families, prioritizing the needs of the planet or the people at large was less important to them. As Protestants, they valued participating in an organized church community. They also valued education, hard work, financial responsibility, family, humor, sociability, and fun. I grew up surrounded by these values, going to church every Sunday (and even singing—quite poorly—in the youth choir!), working hard in school, holding down a job throughout college, prioritizing family and friends, and having loads of fun along the way. As an adult, I still value education, hard work, financial responsibility, family, humor, sociability, and fun. However, my political and spiritual values are quite different from those of my parents and their parish.

As women, we are often encouraged to be agreeable, helpful, deferential, physically presentable, self-sacrificing, and quiet. What messages have you received about the qualities women are supposed to embody? What other messages have you received about how you "should" be? How does this align or contrast with your own ideas of meaningful being and doing?

I have had clients identify service, fitness, or caregiving as values, only to ultimately admit that those were values they thought they "should" have; those values weren't coming from their own hearts and, in some cases, were even serving as avoidance of guilt and shame (for example, "If I don't take care of everyone, all the time, and put myself last, it means I'm a selfish/bad wife, mother, and daughter"). I have had clients who were raised in conservative families, religions, or cultures and who valued sexuality and sensuality, but they struggled to openly admit this, as it was in contrast to what they were taught to value growing up.

As you navigate your own values, consider the many outside influences that may be present as you do so. Then choose, freely, those that are personally meaningful and important to the Me *you* truly wish to be.

VALUES ARE NOT

As important as it is to understand what values are, we also need to clarify what they are not. When I first start unpacking values with my clients, they often initially identify things like "being calm," "being patient," "being confident," "being respected," and "belonging." At first blush, these sound like values. If we call values "qualities of being and doing" then wouldn't "being calm" and the other examples fall under this umbrella? You might think so, but they actually do not. Because values must be qualities of being and doing *that we are actually in charge of.* For something to be a value it has to be something we can actively choose and command—so basically, our mouths, our hands, and our feet. That's it. This can be a little tricky, and it is important to steer clear of the things-that-are-out-of-my-control trap when identifying values. So let's unpack this a bit more by taking a look at what values are *not.*

Values Cannot be Feelings

Values cannot be feelings—we can't "value" feeling calm or feeling patient. Of course, we've all wished that our anxiety or irritability would disappear, and of course, we prefer to feel calm and patient. But what do you now know from your reading thus far? Not only do we not get to control how we feel, we set a trap for the unwillingness paradox when we try (if you are unwilling to have anxiety, you will be anxious about anxiety, so you will have anxiety). If we identify "feeling calm" or "feeling patient" as values, we are essentially saying "I value not having anxiety," thus setting ourselves up to lose a rigged game. Values cannot be feelings because we aren't in charge of what and how we feel.

Instead, we can value things like interacting or communicating respectfully or in a measured way (essentially communicating patience), whether we *feel* calm and patient or not. The same can be said for confidence. We can't value feeling confident (not up to us), though we can value acting boldly (up to us) whether we *feel* confident or not.

Redefining Confidence

"I value being confident" is one of the most common statements I hear from my clients during initial values identification work. If you relate to this, consider what being confident means to you. Many describe it as a *feeling* of self-assurance or conviction along with an absence of self-doubt. If we look to the root of the word "confidence," it is derived from the Latin *con* meaning "with" + *fidere* meaning "trust." So what is trust? Is it assurance? Conviction? Absence of doubt? I would argue it is not. We trust that our partners and friends are being loyal, that our cars will get us to work in one piece, and that the universe is infinite, but we can't *really know* with 100 percent certainty.

When we choose to trust, we are taking a leap of faith. Maybe this is what confidence is really about. We take a leap of faith, choosing to do what matters, even when we're filled with doubt. If, instead, "I want to be more confident" means I have to *feel* self-assured and *not feel* self-doubt, we end up back in an unworkable situation where our futile pursuit of the feelings only results in more stuckness. What we do is under our command, how we feel is not.

If we redefine confidence as doing what matters *with trust* in ourselves and our choices, regardless of how we feel, then it becomes a quality we can choose to embody. It can be a value.

Values Are Not How Others Act

Values cannot be about other people's behavior. For example, you may wish to have others respect you (of course, who doesn't?). However, to say, "I value being respected" sets yet another things-that-are-out-of-your-control trap. Like our own internal experiences, we don't get to control others' thoughts, feelings, or behaviors. So you can value acting respectfully toward others, and this may even make it more likely that others will respect you in turn, but at the end of the day, that is entirely up to them.

Similarly, you may say, "I value belonging." But "belonging," in large part, boils down to whether other people choose to include you in their social circles or not—belonging is not up to you. Instead, you might value being accepting and inclusive of others—how you treat other people is up to you. Once again, this *may* make your own social inclusion more likely, but ultimately, that is not for us to decide.

Irrespective of how others behave toward you (which is not within your control), you can always choose to act respectfully and inclusively toward others (which is within your control). Values are how *you* act, not how others do.

Values Are Not Goals

Values and goals are interrelated, but they are distinct. Specifically, a goal is an outcome, it has an end point; a value does not. A goal can be checked off a to-do list when it's complete; a value cannot. A value is more like an ongoing journey, like traveling west versus going to Hawaii. Or like being healthy (a value—you're never finished being healthy) versus losing ten pounds (a goal—you know when it's complete). In many cultures, we are socialized to focus on goals and outcomes, almost exclusively. However, problems arise when goals dominate our landscape, especially if they exist in the absence of guiding values.

Suppose you decide to climb a mountain with a goal of reaching the summit. There's nothing wrong with setting such a lofty goal, but let's take a closer look, with and without the influence of values.

Let's say you value skillfulness, adventure, and perseverance. You train for your climb for many months, purchase the necessary equipment, and map out the perfect route. When the big day finally arrives, you head off on the trail. Unfortunately, about halfway up, you realize you're not feeling so hot. Not only that, huge, dark clouds have started rolling in, and you realize the wise choice is to turn back. If skillfulness, adventure, and perseverance are your values, what might that mean? Most likely, you will either try the climb on another day (and another after that), or you will persevere through a new adventure. *This doesn't mean you won't feel disappointed or discouraged that your goal wasn't met.* But with your "why" (your values) close by, you will be more likely to keep on keeping on in spite of it.

What if, however, the only thing on your radar was the goal of reaching the summit on that particular day? When your goal gets stymied by sickness and storms, and your "why" isn't nigh, what then? More than likely, you will feel disappointed and discouraged *and* you may give up, never to try again. Similarly, in the absence of values, even if you were to reach the summit, you might decide there is no point in more climbing. Goal achieved, checked off the list, nothing more to be done. Then what?

Last, and perhaps most important (hold on to your hats for this one), goals and outcomes are not really within our control. Values—actions and qualities of actions—*those* we can command. We can train (action) diligently (quality), prepare and plan (actions) thoughtfully (quality), and climb (action) intentionally and mindfully (quality). These values-driven choices may even increase the likelihood that we will get the outcome we desire. But even the best-laid plans succumb to unexpected, uncontrollable complications (like belly aches and bad weather!). Goals in a valueless vacuum can make us feel chronically ineffectual when we define success strictly based on achieving our desired outcomes—outcomes that are bound to elude us a fair amount of the time.

Bring It On: Goals Gone Wild

Before we move on, let's take a minute to make contact with an experience that will allow you to connect these concepts with your own personal experience.

First, grab a pen or pencil or any similar implement you can hold—it doesn't need to write (Stoddard and Afari 2014). Now think about a goal you have been focused on achieving but, as of yet, have been unable to accomplish. This should be something you've been putting a lot of effort into both mentally and physically, but the nature of the goal is such that the outcome isn't entirely up to you. This might be something like landing a job, finding a romantic partner, changing your child's problematic behavior, or getting into graduate school.

You might be engaging in a lot of worry, research, planning, problem solving, venting, or reassurance seeking, while also doing much of what's needed, like completing applications, making phone calls, implementing a behavioral reward system, or joining an online dating community. However, you are getting increasingly frustrated that the outcome you desire remains elusive.

Once you have the details in your mind, take the pen or pencil and grasp it as tightly as would represent all the effort and attention you've been putting into achieving this goal. Notice how hard you're holding the pen; rate it from 0 (as lightly as possible) to 10 (as tightly as possible). Notice how it feels.

Now release your grip so that you are holding the pen at about half of where you just had it (so if you were an 8, hold it at a 4). Notice how that feels, how it has changed, how it feels different from before. Now hold the pen as lightly as possible without letting it drop. Notice how that feels, how it is different from before. What is the one thing that hasn't changed? You are still holding the pen.

Write in your journal about this experience using the following prompts:

* What might your new knowledge around values—what they are and are not—teach you about your experience and the effort you have been putting into achieving this goal? (Hint: what elements are and are not within your personal control?)

* What are your relevant values as they relate to this goal? Why is this important to you?

* How might you focus more on the journey (steps, choices, processes) and hold the outcome a bit more lightly?

* What else might you do, and how, to keep moving forward in ways that matter to you, while holding the outcome more lightly?

To summarize, the risk of being overly focused on goals in the absence of values is:

- If we don't reach a goal, we may decide to give up—even if the value behind it is something very important to us.

- If we reach a goal, we may decide we are done—and then what about the values?

- Outcomes are not within our control—whereas the choices, actions, and steps we take are.

Goals are great—as long as we hold the outcomes lightly and allow our values to illuminate the trail.

Let's look at a real-world example that ties it all together. This example comes straight from my own experience, because, as you may be able to see by now, I genuinely live by the principles you are reading about in this book, principles that have transformed my life in mighty and meaningful ways.

In addition to writing professional psychology books, I like to write personal essays and children's books (chosen actions). The qualities I care about—the Me I want to be—include creativity, courage, perseverance, and skillfulness. I've been writing for about ten years and have a number of pieces at various stages of completion. I've entered a couple into contests and have submitted many to magazines and book publishers; none have won nor been published.

My dream outcome is to win a contest or have something published. Yet, if publication were my only inspiration, I would have given up a long time ago! With my values in charge of my choices, however, I continue to write as a way to be creative (my favorite writing partner!) while I learn about the industry, practice and sharpen my skills, and persevere through rejection after rejection after rejection. It's not easy! It feels terrible!

My Inner Critic laughs at me and tells me I'm an imposter who has no place in creative writing circles. I feel incredibly vulnerable and anxious putting something so personal, something I've created, in front of others for critique. *And* because it deeply matters to me, I'm willing to pull up a few extra chairs at my writing desk for the anxiety, disappointment, and self-doubt; they are my writing partners too. I'm not saying they're my best buds, more like childhood siblings who attempt to torture me and are also a part of my experience I wouldn't want to live without. They are my neon arrows → we hurt where we care. If a crystal ball confirmed today that contest winning and publication would never be in my tomorrow, I would still choose to write.

COMPETING VALUES?

You may be thinking, *I wish I had time to hike up mountains and write personal essays! Maybe I'm just too busy for values* or *How can I be an engaged and loving parent* and *a committed professional?* or *How can I be a loyal friend when school—which is really important to me—takes up so much of my time?* or *How do I handle all these competing values?* But these are not really questions of values, they are questions of balancing time demands across multiple important life domains.

From a strictly values perspective, your values need not compete with one another. When you are in your role of mom, you fully embody engagement and love. When you are in your role of professional, you fully embody commitment. When you are in your role of friend, you fully embody loyalty. And so on. *In this one moment, who is the Me I want to be?* This doesn't mean you will escape guilt when you are at work or school and not with your kids or friends (or vice versa), because balancing time demands between roles that matter to you is hard (as far as I know, no woman has yet mastered the time-demand balancing act in a perfect way that always feels "right" and easy)!

And yet, you can still fully embody your values in whichever role you happen to be in, in this one moment. Engaged, committed, loving, and loyal need not compete, no matter how long your to-do list.

BUT I HAVE REAL PROBLEMS

You may also be thinking, *Girls' night out and being a considerate driver sound nice, but I have real problems, serious things to worry about.* Maybe you are struggling with substance use or compulsive overeating or are estranged from a loved one. Maybe you have limited resources or are caring for sick and aging parents while also caring for young children. There is no end to the list of truly challenging experiences life can throw your way. It can feel overwhelming. And it is *exactly* during these times when you need to connect with the Me you want to be. Values will not magically unveil the "right answer" or "best solution," but they will provide a beacon of light when the world gets dark.

As you pilot your plane through life, despite a carefully crafted flight plan, the sky will get dark, the weather will get stormy, and a bird may even fly into your engine. Hijackers will show up, further attempting to steer you off course with their taunts: "Stop navigating toward health, self-care, and authenticity—you don't deserve it, and who are you kidding, you can't bear cravings or stress; you have no idea how to handle *real* problems."

The hijackers have pushed your detonator, so now what? You could grab your pinot and pizza parachute, abandon your aircraft, and allow it to blow to smithereens. Or you could send a Mayday signal to air traffic control, turn up the volume on your headset, and listen for some wise guidance: "Remember the flyer you admire. Now hold the yoke steady and persevere through the turbulence; pull back with your determination and courage to climb above the storm. Your integrity is illuminating the runway." Air traffic control—your values—will always be there, 24/7/365, to guide you and keep you on course through the roughest of conditions. All you have to do is listen—"10-4, ATC"—and course correct.

Bring It On: Mighty Memoir

Now it's your turn again. A memoir is an up-close and personal account of its narrator's life story. A good memoir provokes us to feel; it moves us to care about the narrator and her journey. We get an intimate sense of who she is, where she came from, what she wants, choices she's made, challenges and obstacles she's encountered, and the resulting growth she experiences.

For this exercise, imagine you have traveled several years into the future and are now preparing to write your memoir. Use your journal to jot down the notes you will use to construct the arc of your life story. You can write in brief bullet points or in full sentences, whichever you prefer.

From your actual lived experience:

* Write about your struggles with anxiety. Write about how you coped with the anxiety, including examples of experiential avoidance, and how this helped give you relief but also got in the way of having the life you wanted.

* Write about that life you wanted, about that person you wanted to be, about the person you knew you could have been if anxiety and avoidance hadn't been getting in the way.

Now, from the perspective of the Me you want to be from the future:

* Write about your growth as you came to realize the importance of making choices that were more consistent with your values, even if that meant anxiety had to come along for the ride. Remember, you are now in the future, looking back, writing your memoir from the perspective of a mighty woman who learned to choose values over avoidance.

* Write about those choices—the things you consciously chose to do differently and the ways you were willing to step outside your Comfort Zone and into the Courage Zone—the place where the magic happens.

* Write about the person who emerged.

What does your memoir tell you about the Me you wish to be—about the values you most want to exemplify your life, your roles, and your general character?

THE TAKEAWAY

You are well on your way toward declaring victory through values! It's time to promote your values to CEO of My Mighty Life Inc. and move desired outcomes to HR (where sometimes the benefits are great and sometimes you get a pink slip).

Harnessing the might of values-based living means choosing the Me you most want to be in this one moment (and the next, and the next) by choosing what you will do (or not do) and how you will do it while holding the outcomes lightly.

We will talk much more in the upcoming pages about *how* to walk this talk when thoughts and fears threaten to get in the way. But we are going to get to know your patterns of thinking and acting a bit better first.

Chapter 6

Understanding Your Suit of Armor

Step out of the history that is holding you back. Step into the new story you are willing to create.

—Oprah Winfrey

We've reached the halfway point and, until now, have been moving along in a pretty linear fashion. In this chapter, we are going to detour into the past, then circle back to the present. Before we divert, let's take a quick minute to recap our journey so far.

- *Psychological flexibility* is our ability to observe and allow all emotional, physical, and sensory experiences as they are, rather than what the mind says they are, fully and without defense, while choosing to do what matters. The concepts presented throughout this book share the same aim of increasing psychological flexibility.

- Struggling to control or minimize internal experiences—*experiential avoidance*—provides brief relief but is ineffective long term and restricts us from having the mighty lives we want.

- *Willingness*, the opposite of experiential avoidance, is the practice of opening to and allowing internal experiences; willingness (also called "acceptance") springs the control trap, so that we may move more freely toward a mightier life.

- *Mindfulness*—purposeful, nonjudgmental, present-moment awareness—is a foundational practice that expands the space between internal experience and reaction. It is in this space where psychological flexibility is brought to life.

- *Values* are the freely chosen, deeply personal qualities of being and doing that define what a mighty life means to each one of us. Values characterize the Me you want to be.

We've covered every ingredient of psychological flexibility, with the exception of thoughts. That's where the next two chapters come in. In this chapter, we are going to uncover the roots of your specific "brand" of thinking—your personal beliefs about yourself, others, and the world—by looking closely at your early life experiences, learning history, and other contextual factors that have impacted you. These personal beliefs, and the patterns of behavior that develop in response to them, make up the chain mail of our suits of armor—the protective covering we don that shields us from pain but makes it hard to move about freely. We will examine the ways in which these beliefs are frequently responsible for pushing your detonators. In chapter 7, we will discuss how to deactivate your well-worn bombs by casting off your suit of armor.

THE IMAGINATIVE MIND

You already know a little bit about the pesky power of thoughts and language. Let's take a moment to review: as vividly as you can, imagine I've just handed you a bright yellow, juicy lemon wedge. Notice the color and texture, the juice dripping down the sides. Now imagine taking a big bite out of that lemon. What do you notice? Puckery cheeks? Extra saliva? And yet, no real lemons. All you had to do was *think* about a lemon and you had a physical response. You may have even noticed thoughts about lemonade, judgments about lemons as being gross or delicious, or even memories tied to an experience with lemons.

This is what minds do. They remember, learn, and make connections—so strongly that the humans who own them experience emotional and physical reactions to what is in the mind, in the absence of actual, in-the-moment experience. This is similar to the way you might feel sad or anxious or begin to cry if you think about losing someone you love, even if that person is safe and sound right in the next room.

Anxiety goes hand in hand with its own special brand of imaginative thinking: worry—those future-oriented what-if thoughts that constantly remind you about all the terrible things that could go wrong. When I initially had the idea for this book, my mind cranked out a spiral of what-ifs: What if the publisher rejects it? What if it's published but no one reads it? What if people read it but think it's terrible? All I had to do was *have an idea* and my mind immediately went to DEFCON 5, filling in all the terrible things that could occur— things that have never actually happened to me—if I chose to move forward. Does this sound familiar? This special brand of cognitive gymnastics is uniquely human.

ANXIOUS BY DESIGN

Humans are the only species capable of making connections in this way—imagining the worst case, even if it has never occurred (Liddell 1949). We are not the only species capable of anxiety. A dog, for example, may experience anxiety during a thunderstorm or when she is left alone. But she is responding to her experience in the present moment. As soon as the thunder stops or her owner returns, her anxiety abates. She never experiences anxiety because she is what-iffing about the future possibility of thunder or abandonment and all the terrible things that could accompany those traumas.

Survival of the Fret-est

Lucky us, right? Actually, in a way, yes. Here's the cool thing: evolutionarily, this makes perfect sense and is one of the reasons we ended up at the top of the food chain. Let's say you are a cavewoman. You wander out of the cave early one morning in search of breakfast. As you forage, you see something off in the distance, but it's a foggy day so you can't quite make out what is up ahead. You say, "Ooh, Ostrich! Yes, please, delicious morning eggs!"

But then your ambiguity alarm sounds: "Hold up! Not so fast! *What if* it's a giant predatory kangaroo?" (Yes, these really existed back then.) If you decide to play it safe, banking on the possibility that it could be a killer kangaroo, you might spend a hungry morning back in your cozy cave. But if you decide to gamble, assuming it's more likely to be a harmless ostrich, you might spend your morning on the monster 'roo's menu.

Evolutionary theory suggests that generalized anxiety likely evolved to manage situations in which the nature of a threat could not be clearly defined (Marks and Nesse 1994) and errors associated with "overresponding" to potential threats were less costly than errors of "underresponding" (Nesse 2001). In other words, the fittest who survived were those who were more likely to perceive threat and play it safe—the "better to be safe than sorry" crew.

It's easy to see, however, that if you habitually turned away from uncertainty and never left the cave, you would eventually die of starvation. So as the evolutionary blueprint advanced, the fittest who survived were likely those who actively sought information to reduce ambiguity. Contemporary research certainly supports this notion and shows that we are hardwired to seek answers and avoid uncertainty (Bromberg-Martin and Hikosaka 2009; de Berker et al. 2016). Let's investigate.

Bring It On: Natural Selection (of a Solution)

For the next thirty to sixty seconds, consider the question "What do a lightbulb and grass have in common?" If an answer appears, no matter the content, jot it down in your notebook. Right or wrong does not matter, just write down anything that comes to mind.

Now reflect on your experience: What did you notice occurring in your mind? At any point after the question was posed, did "I don't know" or "nothing" show up? How long did your mind allow them to stick around? Probably not long. When your brain sees a question mark, it will put its evolutionary adaptations to good use—it will work and work until it comes up with an answer. Rarely will it stay with "I don't know" or "nothing."

Uncertain? Certainly Not!

For cavewomen, ambiguity was public enemy number one. Playing it safe by steering clear of the unknown meant survival. Being able to *figure out* the unknown—whether the figure in the fog actually was an ostrich or a killer kangaroo—not only meant survival, it meant a nice full belly too! As a result, we modern humans inherited a hefty aversion to uncertainty and a strong drive to resolve it. So much so that research has shown we experience less stress in the face of a known threat ("I'm stuck in traffic and will definitely be late for my very important meeting") than in the face of an uncertain one ("Traffic is touch and go, and I may still be on time but am unsure") (de Berker et al. 2015).

Of course, not all uncertainty can be resolved, nor does it need to be for us to be okay. We no longer live with the real possibility that killer kangaroos may be lurking around every corner. So while modern humans inherited a distaste for uncertainty, we also developed an ability to tolerate it. For example, do you read the last page of a new book first? Do you know for sure that your car will deliver you safely to your destination? Over the course of a lifetime, exposure to uncertainty abounds, and acceptance builds each time an uncertain situation is experienced as safe and benign.

But one thing slothlike evolution didn't count on, and can't catch up with, is cheetahlike modern technology. In the age of the Internet, we have constant access to instant answers, right at our fingertips. You want greater certainty about the quality of a dining experience or hair stylist? Just turn to Yelp. In the market for a new hair dryer or wall clock? Look for five stars on Amazon. Before the Internet, we had to wait, we had to take our chances. We sat with uncertainty all the time. And we learned. Either the hair dryer turned out just fine or, if it didn't, it was no big deal and we handled it.

Once Siri and Alexa came along to answer all our most burning questions, the very moment we had them, we got hooked on immediate gratification. And what exactly is that gratification? Relief from uncertainty—the more of which we get, the more of which we need. Yelp restaurant reviews are like a gateway drug to WebMD. Why sit with not knowing the reason you've felt so tired the past couple days, when you can just ask Dr. Internet? But what happens when you turn to WebMD for a fix? A moment of relief as you get some answers, followed quickly by the realization that you now have many more questions, coupled with new worries that you might have congestive heart failure or leukemia, topped off with a dose of urgency that you best get to your real doctor, stat! The cycle of anxious uncertainty goes on and on.

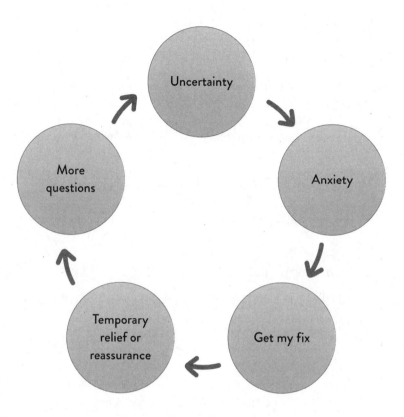

Bring It On: What's Your Fix?

Let's take a moment to connect the cycle of anxious uncertainty to your personal experience. In your journal, reflect on the role of uncertainty in your life.

* Where does uncertainty show up, and what do you do in response?

* Where do you turn for reassurance—what's your fix?

* How might technology play a role?

* What does this get you (e.g., temporary relief) and what is the cost?

* Does your fix really work, or are you soon going through withdrawal, jonesing for another hit?

* Does this bring you closer to or farther from your values?

Keep this information nearby, as it may come in handy as we unpack your suit of armor later in this chapter.

Technology has deleted many of our opportunities to master living with uncertainty. In the absence of practice, tolerating uncertainty becomes increasingly more difficult. And struggling to tolerate uncertainty has been linked to higher levels of anxiety (Carleton 2016).

Lions and Friends and Skunks, Oh My!

Think about the things you tend to worry about most. Do they have anything in common? If humans lived solitary lives—with no friends, partners, family members, kids, supervisors, colleagues, or roommates—would our worries change? I'm guessing you don't worry much about being hunted for food, but I bet you do worry about things connected to the social world.

Early humans who hunted, gathered, and traveled in groups had many survival advantages compared to those who remained solitary (Nesse 1998). We didn't have the speed of lions, the teeth of tigers, or the claws of bears. We had each other. We evolved to need each other, to be social beings. In one of the world's longest longitudinal studies, the single most important predictor of health and well-being across the adult lifespan was the presence of high-quality relationships (Waldinger 2015).

And do you know how researchers study the effects of antidepressants in social animals who are thought to be similar to humans? They can't recruit depressed rats by posting fliers at Rodent University; they have to *make* the rats depressed. They do so simply by isolating them (Wilson 2018).

Connections matter! So now we worry about what others think and whether we measure up (and social media has become a toxic "fix"). We worry about the well-being of the people we care about. If we don't worry about these things, we might end up alone (or at least that's what our primitive minds tell us), and evolution has programmed our brains to understand that to be alone is to be extinguished. That's some pretty heavy stuff! But it also means that worry and caring about the group are hallmarks of being human.

These are not pathologies that need to be eradicated. If that had been the case, evolution would have selected it out long ago, or we'd be seeing decreasing levels of worry and social comparison over time, rather than the increases that have actually occurred.

Suppose a skunk came to you and said, "I have a terrible, horrible problem and I desperately need your help! Every so often, especially when I get scared, my butt makes a disgusting, foul, and embarrassing odor. It's so bad, it sends everyone running for the hills. Something is seriously wrong with me. You've got to help me fix it!" What would you say to the skunk? Most likely, "Um, you're a skunk. There's nothing wrong with you, all skunks have that. In fact, it's what keeps you safe from predators. If that stink didn't send them running for the hills, they'd eat you. It's not a problem that needs to be fixed, it's just a helpful part of you that makes you you."

All skunks have a smelly spray, and that spray is adaptive. The same is true for humans' worries and social comparisons. We all have them and they are designed to protect us, to keep us in good standing with our tribes. Our worries are not problems to be fixed, they are a part of us that makes us us. However, in much the same way a skunk only sprays when in danger, we can learn to respond to only what is needed in the moment. If a skunk senses no danger, he doesn't spray. If our worries are not going to serve us, we can choose to acknowledge their presence and move on (more on *how* in chapter 7), choosing valued actions rather than heeding their warnings. Cavewomen who listened to every worry and never stepped outside the comfort of their caves were excluded from the group, didn't procreate, and starved to death.

SUITS OF ARMOR

We arrive in the world evolutionarily programmed to see threat, resolve uncertainty, and worry about our relationships. We are additionally molded by our interactions with the prominent people in our lives, cultural circumstances under which we live, and significant specific events we experience. Our efforts to interpret and make sense of these life experiences in a meaningful way result in the development of a set of *core beliefs*, or *schemas*, we hold about ourselves, other people, and the world (Beck 1967; Young, Klosko, and Weishaar 2003). Core beliefs might be things such as, *I am incompetent*, *People can't be trusted*, or *The world is unsafe.*

Core beliefs can be positive or negative, though for the purposes of understanding your suit of armor, we will be focusing primarily on your negative beliefs. We will also use the terms "schema," "belief," "core belief," "personal belief," and "thought" interchangeably.

Schemas lead to patterns of behavior that are often adaptive or protective at the time they develop (Young, Klosko, and Weishaar 2003). For example, an abused child who develops the belief *People I love will hurt me* might make herself scarce around an abusive parent, effectively reducing her exposure to harm. As adults, we continue to apply the same "logic" even if it no longer makes sense in the current environment (Young, Klosko, and Weishaar 2003), and those once-protective behaviors serve to reinforce and maintain the schemas. So that same abused child who avoided her parent as a survival tactic may, as an adult, withdraw from or avoid true closeness with friends or romantic partners, even though her circumstances have changed. This will likely give her a sense of safety and control (so these behaviors still feel protective), but her detachment in relationships will invariably lead to relationship demise, reinforcing the belief that *People I love will hurt me*. And the cycle goes on and on.

These core beliefs and patterns of behavior, or "safety behaviors," make up our suits of armor—the protective shell we hide behind to shield ourselves from pain. But it limits our ability to move about freely and fully. When we notice our detonators have been pressed, schemas are often part of the activation; the safety behaviors we pull out in response are the exploding bombs.

In this chapter, we are going to inspect your suit of armor so you can become a keen observer of its presence and the ways it might be restricting your movement. To start, let's look at an example of a woman I worked with in my anxiety clinic.

Sepidah's Story

Sepidah grew up with a highly critical mother. In her mother's eyes, nothing Sepidah did was ever good enough—every choice she made was wrong, and every challenge she faced was her fault. If she made time to exercise, her mother would criticize her for taking time away from her family. If she didn't exercise, her mother would criticize her for not taking care of herself. She even went so far as to blame Sepidah for the death of her own father (which she had absolutely nothing to do with and, in fact, she was an important point person in his care).

No matter what Sepidah did, she couldn't win. She could never please her mother. She kept trying to understand the expectations so she could win her mother's approval, but the goalposts were moved every time. On top of that, Sepidah lived in three different countries, all with very different cultures, further adding to the self-doubt around how she was "supposed" to be.

Sepidah felt anxious, confused, and helpless. She longed for certainty so that she might know what to do and how to do it, to gain the approval she craved, and to have some small sense of control. She developed two main beliefs that continuously appeared in her life: *If I don't do what others want/expect/need, something bad will happen* (they will reject me, they will blame me, harm will befall them, harm will befall me), and *The rules for doing what others want/expect/need* (and therefore for preventing bad things from happening) *are unclear.*

Behaviorally, Sepidah was a classic people-pleaser. She was always "nice" and constantly apologizing, even when she hadn't done anything wrong. As a wife and mother, she did everything for everyone and left herself completely off the to-do list. In areas entirely outside her control, she developed her own rules and corresponding superstitious avoidance strategies and compulsive rituals aimed at preventing harm (not driving by the house of someone who had died of a terminal illness, wearing only certain clothing, not throwing away certain items—all to increase good energy or decrease bad energy).

Sepidah's safety behaviors gave her a sense of certainty, predictability, and control, and reduced her fear of rejection and harm. However, she felt chronically anxious and somewhat resentful. Her family members were very demanding of her and rebelled anytime she requested that they contribute.

Her suit of armor ultimately re-created the powerlessness she was trying to avoid when her rituals took up more and more space in her life and failed to prevent painful experiences. And her beliefs that *Bad things happen when I fail to please others* and *The rules for doing what others want/expect/need* (and therefore for preventing bad things from happening) *are unclear* were maintained and reinforced.

Using Sepidah as a model, let's try to understand what makes up your personally tailored suit of armor. What we are ultimately trying to piece together is:

- The early experiences of hurt and unmet emotional needs that impacted the development of your schemas

- The content of your specific beliefs about yourself, others, and the world

- The things you do or don't do (safety behaviors) when these beliefs get activated

- How these behaviors both protect you *and* make it harder to move freely, ultimately reinforcing and mainting unhelpful schemas

Bring It On: Part I—The Sword and the Helmet

In your journal, write about your childhood and adolescent experiences. Describe what it was like growing up in your family.

How many adults raised you? Give details of marriages, divorces, deaths; full, step-, and half-relatives; and so forth.

What were your parents or primary caregivers like? Were they involved, MIA, loving, critical, strict, supportive, demanding, permissive, overprotective, abusive, struggling with a medical or mental illness?

Write about experiences outside your family that may be important: bullying, cultural influences (race, ethnicity, gender, sexuality, military), learning or other disabilities, moving around a lot, losses, other trauma, protective factors such as loving or supportive mentors or extended family members, finacial security, healthy friendships.

Reflect and write about what you wanted, needed, or desperately longed for but didn't get. Describe how this made you feel. Connect these unmet needs to your early experiences from above and write about the hurt around this. For example, you may remember longing for acceptance and unconditional love from your parents, but instead they were highly critical of your grades, appearance, or perceived "mistakes"; this made you feel worthless and lonely. These early hurts are the sword.

Write about other messages you received growing up. For example, if you had an anxious, overprotective parent who worried about your safety and refused to let you go to the mall with your friends or ride your bike to school, you might interpret this as a message that *The world is dangerous and the people in it are either predators or vulnerable victims.* If you grew up with a neglectful, uninvolved caregiver who didn't show up to your sporting events, didn't help you with homework, or didn't ask about your whereabouts for entire weekends, you might interpret this as a message that *People are meant to survive on their own and family is unimportant.*

Reflect on the lingering impact your experiences, your unmet needs, and the messages you received have had on you: specifically, write down some of the schemas or beliefs that developed as a result of your efforts to make sense of your experiences and environment. These beliefs are the helmet.

You might use some or all of the following to help get you started:

I am _____ [unlovable, fragile, invisible].

I am not _____ [smart, attractive, capable, important].

I should/must/ought to _____ [be perfect, take precautions, be self-sufficient].

People are _____ [judgmental, cruel, out for themselves].

People are not _____ [forgiving, trustworthy, supportive].

The world is _____ [cutthroat, dangerous, anonymous].

The world is not _____ [easily navigable, safe, providing].

If I _____ [try my best, take risks, rely on others]
then _____ [it still won't be good enough, I will get
hurt, they will let me down].

_____ [Making mistakes, Putting myself in uncertain situations, Asking for support] means _____
[I'm defective, I'm asking for trouble, I'm weak].

In a general sense, schemas allow us to organize and process information about our environment (Beck 1967). When core emotional
needs (safety, love, or care) go unmet during childhood, negative
schemas result from our attempts to make sense of these experiences
(Young, Klosko, and Weishaar 2003).

As adults, we maintain our schemas, even if they are no longer
applicable. When schemas are triggered, we respond with safety
behaviors—behaviors that were likely adaptive during youth but cease
to remain so over time. In practice, these safety behaviors even serve
to maintain negative beliefs.

Bring It On: Part II—The Suit and the Shield

Reflect back on your painful childhood and adolescent experiences
(the sword of early hurts), the ways you made sense of those experiences, and the beliefs that developed as a result (the schema helmet).
Consider some of the things you did when those schemas first developed. Identify some of the things you do now when these beliefs
show up.

Write down your past and present behaviors in your journal.
You might notice things such as perfectionism, people-pleasing, situational avoidance, substance use, or refusing to ask for help.

Write about how these behaviors were adaptive during childhood. How did they protect you? These are your suit and shield. For

example, if you had a highly critical parent, you may have developed the belief *I should avoid mistakes at all costs,* along with corresponding perfectionistic behaviors that likely would have reduced the criticism you had to endure at that time.

Write about how these same safety behaviors may be less adaptive now. What costs do they have? In what ways does this part of your armor restrict your movement? Using the same example, perhaps as an adult, you avoid new or challenging tasks at work, knowing you will fail to accomplish them perfectly. Perhaps you turn in projects late because you spend too much time perfecting the details.

Finally, write about how these behaviors backfire by re-creating the exact early hurts they were designed to protect you from. Write about how this process maintains the schema. For example, avoiding new work tasks or failing to turn in projects by a deadline will very likely result in criticism from your supervisor or colleagues. This will reinforce your belief that you should avoid mistakes at all costs.

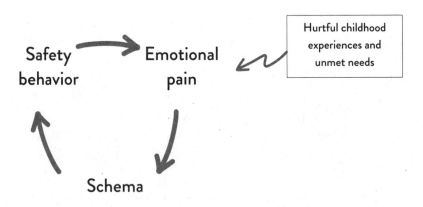

Let's look at two additional examples to help deepen your understanding.

Alison's Story

Alison grew up in a culture and family in which women were stereotyped as holding grudges and being "catty" and "ruthless" toward other women, and men were credited with being able to let things go. Alison wanted to feel a safe bond with her mom but frequently heard her "smack talking" women behind their backs right after interacting with them in a loving and positive way; Alison never observed her father acting inauthentically with his friends. Her mom also shared things with others (in a gossipy way) that Alison had asked her to keep private. This left her feeling hurt, anxious, alone, and disconnected.

Alison developed the belief If I trust women and get close, they will betray me. *Alison surrounded herself with mostly male friends and kept female relationships superficial. These behaviors gave her a sense of safety and control. However, her suit of armor prevented her from bonding with women, thereby re-creating the hurt of feeling alone and disconnected that she had been trying to avoid. Her detached and superficial behavior toward women led them to exclude her, reinforcing her belief that if she trusts or gets close to women, they will betray her.*

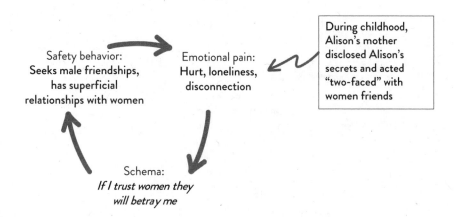

Safety behavior:
Seeks male friendships, has superficial relationships with women

Emotional pain:
Hurt, loneliness, disconnection

During childhood, Alison's mother disclosed Alison's secrets and acted "two-faced" with women friends

Schema:
If I trust women they will betray me

Heidi's Story

Heidi wanted her parents to trust and believe in her, but they controlled all her decisions, dictated her schedule, and fixed all her problems. Heidi was raised during a time when parenting culture focused on hyperscheduling kids and pushing obstacles out of the way in an effort to protect children from pain, frustration, and failure. While Heidi felt loved and supported, she also experienced high anxiety and self-doubt about her competence. She developed the belief If I try to figure things out on my own, I will fail.

Heidi constantly looked to others to take the lead—to choose restaurants or movies or make the birthday plans. This safety behavior helped her avoid the crippling self-doubt that decisions triggered in her; it also protected her from making "wrong" decisions and "failing." However, when Heidi was confronted with unstructured time and had no one else to take the lead, she became paralyzed, not knowing what she "should" do.

Her suit of armor caused her to feel even more anxiety and self-doubt, and ultimately created a sense of failure when she "wasted" entire days that she could have devoted to studying, exercising, or recreation. This reinforced and maintained her belief that she was incapable of figuring things out independently.

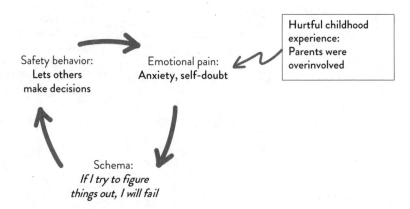

Continue to hammer together the plates that compose your suit of armor. Return to your journal as new ideas emerge (which they are bound to do!). You can also find a fillable Suit of Armor Cycle at http://www.newharbinger.com/34413.

IT'S NOT YOUR FAULT

We don't choose our parents, our childhoods, or our evolutionary histories. We don't choose sexism, racism, or trans/homophobia. We come by our beliefs and protective behaviors honestly—they make sense, given the context, and they work, at least a little.

Where you have arrived is not your fault.

But it is your responsibility: your responsibility to notice your beliefs and choose how to respond when they get activated; your responsibility to cast off your suit of armor when it is not serving you (*how* to shed your armor is the topic of chapter 7). There is freedom in this! You no longer have to be beholden to your history.

THE TAKEAWAY

Anxiety can be tough. But it's not your fault that you have it. We evolved to think up what-ifs, to resolve uncertainty, and to ensure our place in the tribe. Our tolerance of uncertainty muscles have atrophied as technology has found its way into nearly every corner of our lives. Our early experiences of hurt emerge as beliefs and behaviors aimed at protecting us from further hurts. Threaded together, we sew a thick suit of armor, just trying to survive all the potential threats out there. But the tradeoff for feeling safe is more of what we're trying to get away from and less of what we truly desire.

This complex amalgam of the stuff that makes us us is exactly what shows up to push our detonators. Nonjudgmental awareness of the suit of armor beliefs and hurts will help unlock the space between detonator and bomb. Willingness to feel the pain, and casting the armor aside through defusion, will be other tools (provided in the upcoming chapter) to deactivate the bomb. Next time your detonator is activated, and the bomb explodes, see if your suit of armor was the thing to push the button.

Chapter 7

Casting Off Your
Suit of Armor

*And the day came when the risk to remain tight in a bud
was more painful than the risk it took to blossom.*

—Anaïs Nin

Have you ever tried to talk yourself out of your thoughts? To "just
think positive"? It turns out our schemas aren't very amenable to dele-
tion or revision. Brains can't erase what they've already learned, they
can only add new information (Bouton 2014). But the good news is
that beliefs don't need to change or disappear to stop the trouble they
are capable of causing. So you can stop trying so hard to blow sunshine
up your own you-know-what (which only makes you feel more broken
when you fail to believe your own hype).

Instead of changing the content of the schemas that compose our
suits of armor, we can learn to change our relationship to them. We
can decide how much power we will allow them to wield. We can learn
a new way of responding—a psychologically flexible way—when these
beliefs invariably show up (McKay, Lev, and Skeen 2012). This is how
we will begin to cast off our suits of armor.

Recalling the women from the previous chapter, Heidi can worry about failure, and take the lead anyway—in the service of developing independence. Alison can believe women will betray her, and nevertheless choose to let them in—in the service of connection. Sepidah can predict that her family will be angry with her, and still ask them to contribute to the household—in the service of self-respect.

BANISHING BANISHMENT

How much power do your thoughts currently possess? Does your mind act like a dictator in deciding what you will and will not do, and how you will or will not do it? If so, it's time for a coup! How do we overthrow a tyrannical ruler? We will get to that momentarily. But first, let's talk about what not to do.

It may feel tempting to try tossing the dictator into the dungeon and throwing away the key. But I suspect you've already tried this. How successful have you been when you've attempted to banish the anxious, doubting, or negative thoughts that plague you? Does the dictator pipe down for good, or does she end up shouting more loudly, banging on the bars, and continuing to order you around? Extensive research has shown that the harder we try to push away our thoughts, the more present and powerful they become (Wegner 1994; Wenzlaff and Wegner 2000). Let's investigate.

Bring It On: Just Stop Thinking About it

Right now, I want you to try as hard as you possibly can to not think about a thunderstorm (Hayes and Smith 2005). Don't picture the dark sky, the gray clouds, or flashes of lightning; don't hear the driving rain or loud cracks of thunder. Whatever you do, just don't think about it. Maybe you can try thinking of something else to help you. Instead of thinking about a thunderstorm, think about a rainbow in its place. Picture the pretty array of red, orange, yellow, green, blue, indigo, and violet. Spend the next minute doing whatever it takes to not think about a thunderstorm and to think of the rainbow instead.

When the minute is up, reflect on your experience in your journal. What did you notice? Were you successful? Most people notice small portions of time not thinking about the thunderstorm, but pushing those thoughts away requires a lot of effortful attention and it doesn't last. The clouds and rain often begin to compete with the rainbow. In fact, every time you do a quick mental check to see if it's working—*Am I successfully not thinking about the thunderstorm?*—the check causes you to think of the storm that you're trying not to think about!

Attempts to banish the thoughts we don't like tend to fail miserably. Instead, we can respond to thoughts as we might respond to having a song stuck in our head. Whether we like the song or not, the more we try to force it away by not thinking about it, or by playing a different tune to replace it, the more power we give it and the longer it tends to linger.

So when does a sticky song finally fade? When we just let it play in the background and let go of the struggle to get rid of it. The song may well return or be replaced by another annoying song, but letting go of the struggle to silence it frees it to move about. In this way, the song (and similarly our thoughts) can move through our minds like a fried egg on a nonstick pan. The harder we try to push the thoughts away, the more stuck-on they become. Don't just believe me, test it out. Ask Alexa to play "Baby Shark" and spend half the day trying to force it out of your head. For the second half, do the opposite. (I'm so sorry for mentioning the song that shall not be named. If it makes you feel any better, it's in my head now too.)

CASTING OFF BY CONNECTING

We can't forcefully banish unwanted thoughts once they arise, nor can we stop them from showing up in the first place. Events trigger schemas, and schemas create a lens through which we filter our experience (Roediger, Stevens, and Brockman 2018). We don't get to choose the internal experiences we have, but we can choose to respond in ways that diminish their authority and allow us to move about our lives more freely. One way to cast off the suit of armor schema is through three points of connection (Roediger, Stevens, and Brockman 2018):

1. **Connect to the story.** Become an aware observer of the presence of the schema.

2. **Connect to the past.** Link what you are thinking and feeling in the present to what you experienced and felt in the past. Notice how the triggered story is "old" but is still intruding on you today.

3. **Connect to the present.** Identify your current values and consider what alternative action—in place of the habitual suit of armor defense—is needed to move you toward the life you want.

Stepping Up by Stepping Back

To successfully complete the steps above, we have to contact our *observing selves*. Take a moment, right now, to notice the sensations of your feet in your shoes or resting on the floor or furniture. Now also notice who is noticing them. Are you the sensations in your feet? Or are you the one who is aware of those sensations? There is a You who has sensations but is also separate from them. This is your observing self (Luoma, Hayes, and Walser 2007).

You have thoughts, emotions, sensations, memories, and urges, but You are not those things. There is a stable, unchanging You who can step back and observe these ever-changing experiences in a curious and detached way. You can watch your thoughts and stories without being hooked and dragged around by their content.

Look around and pick up anything that is nearby. If there's nothing around, you can use the ring on your finger, the watch or bracelet on your wrist, or the bottom of the shirt you're wearing. Hold it up to your eyes as close as you can without hurting yourself. Now, without moving it, describe the object in detail. And now, keeping it right where it is, in front of your eyes, describe the rest of your surroundings. What do you notice? Kind of tough, right? And what if you now tried to stand up and navigate around the room with the object still close to your eyes? This is what it's like when we get caught up in our thoughts and stories—we can't see beyond them, and our options for action are pretty narrow.

Now take the object and hold it at arm's length, or place it in your lap. How does your ability to describe the object and your surroundings change? How does your ability to move about change? This is the shift we want to make with our thoughts.

Imagine throwing a parade to celebrate your successful cognitive coup. As you sit comfortably on your balcony, you watch and wave to the many parade floats cruising by: there goes the what-if float, followed by "I'm not good enough," with "Bad things are going to happen" bringing up the rear. You are not riding on the float, you are not directing the traffic, and you are not controlling the speed of the parade. You are safe on the sideline, watching and noticing each float as it moves past you.

When you are *on* the float, you have no choice but to be taken along for its ride, whether it's heading in a valued direction or not. When you are on the balcony, you can see *all* the floats, including the "I want to be adventurous" float and the "Creativity matters" float. From this observer perspective you can flexibly shift your attention, within each moment, and consciously choose to do what matters, *whether the schema lines up with that choice or not.* In this way, you can exchange your suit of armor for a cape of psychological flexibility, letting go of unhelpful defenses and flying toward the mighty life you want.

Watching your thoughts as parade floats is just one option for practicing stepping back and observing your thoughts. Get creative here! You can play with your own unique experiential ways for shifting your perspective from one where you are caught up in thoughts to one where you are standing back and looking at them, from a distance, with curiosity.

If you love to watch CNN or you follow the financial markets, you might imagine your thoughts as a news or stock ticker. If you are a sports fan, you might imagine yourself as a spectator and your thoughts as different elements of the sporting event. If you like aviation, you might think of your thoughts being skywritten by a plane or placed on a banner being pulled behind one. In each case, you are standing back as a separate observer, dispassionately watching your thoughts as they arise, and allowing them to move freely, without bringing you along for their ride. Try different practices on for size and see how it goes.

Watch out any time you find yourself saying, "It didn't work." What does it mean to "work?" None of the practices in this book are meant to make your thoughts or feelings go away. We are not trying to change your internal experiences; we are trying to change your *relationship* to them. Stepping back and observing is intended to diminish the authority of your thoughts (not diminish the presence of the thoughts themselves), creating more space for values-driven choosing.

FUSION

Thoughts are a funny thing. We've already talked about lemons and chalkboards and worries and how humans have an odd superpower of being able to imagine the worst catastrophes in the absence of direct experience. But in reality, thoughts themselves are not actually powerful. Their power is granted by the meaning we assign them. Let's take a closer look at this.

Bring It On: The Might Is in the Meaning

In your journal, create two columns. At the top of the first column, write "Thought." At the top of the second column, write "Distress 0–10." Alternatively, you can find a convenient, downloadable worksheet with these columns at http://www.newharbinger.com/34413 if you'd rather make it easier on yourself.

1. In column 1, under Thought, write "The sky is blue." Next to that, in column 2, rate how distressed you feel (0 to 10, with 0 being not at all distressed, and 10 being extremely distressed) as you write or think "The sky is blue."

2. In column 1, below "The sky is blue," write "I want my best friend to die" and then rate your distress in column 2.

3. Next, in column 1 write, "Ma tahan, et mu parim sõber sureb" and again rate your distress in column 2.

4. Now write "I really hope my best friend dies" in column 1, and rate your distress in column 2.

5. Finally, write "I eallyray opehay eyemay estbay riendfay iesday" in column 1, and rate your distress in column 2.

As you look at your numbers and observe how you feel, what do you notice? Did you feel more distressed when you were thinking about best-friend death wishes? Maybe you noticed a bit of a gut-punch sensation. But thinking it doesn't make it true, nor does is it compel you to act.

"I want my best friend to die" is a string of letters, syllables, and sounds, just like "the sky is blue" is a string of different letters, syllables, and sounds. "Ma tahan, et mu parim sõber sureb" is "I want my best friend to die" in Samoan; "I eallyray opehay eyemay estbay

riendfay iesday" is "I really hope my best friend dies" in nonsensi-
cal Pig Latin. If you didn't recognize these languages, your distress
level was probably similar to thinking "the sky is blue." If you caught
on to the Pig Latin, you may have even felt amused. The might is in
the meaning you assign.

The point here is that thoughts are not in themselves problematic.
It is when we become *fused* with their literal content—buying into
thoughts as truths, assigning meaning, following rules or reasons, and
jumping to action, even if that action moves us away from our values—
that problems of inflexibility arise (Hayes, Strosahl, and Wilson 1999).

When Heidi is fused with "If I take charge, I will fail" she becomes
inert and loses contact with the Me she wants to be. However, when
she *defuses,* she separates from the content of thoughts, contacts her
observing self, and flexibly chooses a values-directed option: making
her own choices in the service of being independent.

Fun with Fusion

So how else can we defuse from thoughts? We can step back and
observe them like floats in a parade or daily stories on a news ticker.
We can say them in another language. We can even sing them in a
song (Hayes and Smith 2005). Let's try that one. Pick one of your
pesky thoughts that bothers you (even better if it's one that leads to
unworkable action). Then pick a song, like "Mary Had a Little Lamb,"
only sing it (enthusiastically, please!) with your name instead of Mary's
and replace "little lamb" with some element of your thought. I have a
client (whose name I have changed here) whose song goes like this:
"Lolly had a great big butt, great big butt, great big butt! Lolly had a
great big butt, whose width was wide as Wichita. And everywhere that
Lolly went… [you get the idea], her butt was sure to go!"

What do you notice as you sing your song?

These practices are not meant to be invalidating of the pain that
comes with thinking. They are to put you in direct contact with the

experience that the might is in the meaning we assign. When we can pull back and see thoughts for what they are, rather than getting caught up in them as if they are Gospel Truths, we can better see our behavioral options and choose to respond flexibly.

So try some of these on for size too: What if you say your thought in a wacky voice? What if you picture it like the wizard in Oz, big and mean and loud and commanding? But then you pull back the curtain and see that powerless imposter for what it really is—just a small group of sounds and syllables trying to pull your levers and push your buttons by sounding mean, scary, and commanding. Or just say it as fast as you can ten times (bigbuttbigbuttbigbuttbigbuttbigbuttbigbuttbigbuttbig buttbigbuttbigbutt).

Hooked on Thinking

Another way to talk about fusion is to say we "get hooked" by our thoughts. When we are fused with thoughts, we get hooked by them in much the same way a fish gets hooked on a fly. A good fly-fisher knows exactly what the specific fish in a specific river are feeding on and ties up flies that imitate those insects (Stoddard and Afari 2014). She casts the fly into the stream right in front of the fish, and the fish sees it floating by, buys into the belief that the fly is real, bites it, and gets hooked.

Our thoughts are like specific flies the fisherwoman-mind designs—your fly-thoughts are different from mine, and ours are different from others'—and our minds carefully choose exactly the thoughts we'll bite on. The mind casts them out on the stream in front of us, and the fly-thoughts seem so real that we buy into them, bite, and get hooked.

Once we're hooked, the more we struggle, the more we behave in ways that drive the hook in deeper; this keeps us stuck on the line, inhibiting our journey upstream.

As we swim in the river of life, there are flies floating by on the surface all the time. As we get better at spotting flies and recognizing that we don't have to bite them all, we get hooked less often and have more flexibility to swim in the direction of our values.

Sometimes we will choose to bite—the point is not to ignore all thoughts as value-driven life-killers but to consciously select our responses based on whether a thought is helpful in moving us closer to the life we want. If you think, *My interview is next week, I need to research the organization and buy a snappy suit*, listening to the content of that thought and choosing to prepare is a flexible choice, assuming you value presenting yourself professionally at an interview. If you think, *My interview is next week, there's no way I'm qualified for this position and I'm doomed to bomb the interview*, listening to the content of that thought could derail you from your professional path in a number of unworkable ways.

Bring It On: Retooling the Inner PEBS

Remember the very first exercise we did, whereby you listened to your inner Potential-Emergency Broadcast System warning you about everything that might go wrong? As promised, we are returning to that exercise to take a look at how being fused with your inner PEBS impacts your life.

Turn back to that first exercise and look over the worries you recorded. Add any additional warnings that have joined the chorus, including the beliefs you identified in constructing your suit of armor.

* With your new understanding of fusion and defusion, reflect on the ways your relationship to these beliefs has moved you closer to or farther from the life you want, up to this point. When you assign meaning, follow rules, or assume that the warnings or beliefs are valid or true, what occurs?

* If you step back and observe these thoughts like floats in a parade, hear them as sounds and syllables, open your-

self to discomfort, and consider the life you want and the Me you want to be, how might your choices change or stay the same?

* Now imagine you have a bunch of helium balloons—one for each worry or belief you've written down. Then cut the knot off one of your balloons and deeply inhale the gas into your lungs. Read each of your inner PEBS warnings and suit of armor beliefs as Helium Girl: sillier than a silly goose, more powerful than fusion, voice able to leap higher than tall buildings in a single inhale!

* Reflect on how Helium Girl has the might to defuse your inner PEBS, shed your suit of armor, and strengthen your powers of psychological flexibility.

* Now imagine writing each of your inner PEBS warnings and suit of armor beliefs on your remaining helium balloons, one thought per balloon. One by one, release a balloon and watch it float into the sky. Notice how you remain a grounded observer; how you have thoughts but are separate from them. Reflect on how this defused stance might dissolve your suit of armor and make you more mighty.

* Notice any thoughts or feelings related to watching the balloons "go away."

Even knowing all that you now know about the costs of experiential avoidance and cognitive control, you may still naturally fantasize about your pain floating off into space. This is, of course, perfectly natural, and also not the purpose of this exercise. If you take note of your experience, you will find that even if your thoughts fade, they typically return. It is your job to practice defusing from them each and every time.

GROWING THICKER SKIN

As you infuse ACT into your life more and more, I think you will find it is so mighty-making that it just gets in your bones. What follows is an intimate first-person account of one fierce psychologist's journey—my friend and colleague who has ACT in her bones—from anxious self-condemnation to acceptance and self-love, using defusion in ACT.

Shoshana's Story

I used to stare at my skin intently, wishing it could grow thicker. Or at the very least, wishing I could zip it off and walk around without it absorbing so much suffering. In graduate school, a fellow therapist and friend told me that I needed to not be so sensitive; he looked me square in the eyes and directed me to "Grow thicker skin!"

"How?!" I asked.

He said I just needed to not care so much and just get over my anxious feelings and worry. Truthfully, I agreed; I thought I just needed to shut down and not feel my feelings anymore. The premise behind this idea was that I was letting something seemingly small and irrelevant bother me. When I bought into the notion that a simple change in my mind-set would fix my anxiety, the opposite experience occurred: it drove up my worries further than before. I then became anxious about being anxious.

Why could I not see another way? Because I was fully fused to my self-critic. There was no separation between myself and my thoughts. Growing thicker skin seemed like a decent idea because I didn't want to be me; the "me" I knew was anxious, and my mind was fused to the idea that it was bad to feel anxious. Therefore, I thought I needed to erase the anxiety. I accepted my thoughts as absolute truths, and this fusion left no space to do anything other than carry out what they commanded.

When the command "Grow thicker skin!" filtered through the perspective of my self-critic, this is what I heard:

- "Get over myself, quick. My feelings don't matter."

- "I need to acquire something on the outside of my body to be whole and to navigate this situation."

- "There must be something wrong with me."

- "Don't examine what's bothering me. Put up another layer instead."

Around the same time that I was formulating a plan to grow thicker skin, I went to my first ACT workshop, where I learned about cognitive defusion. We were asked to do an exercise called "Taking Your Mind for a Walk" [Hayes, Strosahl, and Wilson 1999]. I partnered up with my friend; in the exercise I was myself and she was my mind. We linked arms and happily walked around the auditorium. She told me to go left, and I went left. She told me to pick up a piece of paper, and I picked it up. She told me to go right, to go in circles, to stand on one leg, when to stop, and when to go. I was nailing this exercise! Or so I thought...

After ten minutes of me being a dutiful servant, my partner finally leaned over to me and whispered, "You know, you don't have to follow everything I say." I had completely missed the whole point of the exercise. It never even occurred to me to not do what the person (i.e., my self-critic, a.k.a. my mind) was telling me to do. She had to tell me not to follow her, and I felt so embarrassed and confused. Why would I not do what my thoughts told me to do? Why would I ever question that strategy?

The more I learned about ACT, the more I began to see how useful cognitive defusion was. For one thing, it took a whole lot of pressure off of me. I could identify my thoughts as separate from myself and my emotions, and I could recognize that these thoughts were generated by my mind. I no longer had to prove or disprove the validity of my thoughts or follow them into impossible situations. And I started to wonder, How does one actually grow thicker skin anyway? Maybe I had just the right thickness of skin.

What if my struggle had nothing to do with the outside at all?
As Anne Lamott [2017] says, "It's an inside job."

I think famous nineteenth-century abolitionist and author Harriet Beecher Stowe summed it up perfectly: "Sensitive people never like the fatigue of justifying their instincts" [1856, 33]. The reality was, and still is, that I didn't need to add layers to my skin at all. To do so would have made things worse because, in the process, I would have been dismissing my instincts. I actually had just the right thickness of skin. It was really about embracing my inside—dark parts and all—but in a non-vortex, cognitively defused kind of way. I needed to gently unfold the layers and do a deeper allowing of what was bothering me inside my body.

These days, I practice ACT and mindfulness on a daily basis, and I have come to embrace my skin and my anxiety. It has enabled me to make meaningful changes in my personal and professional life; more specific, it has helped guide me to be a better therapist, friend, parent, adult, and partner.

If anything, the only regret I have related to my skin is that I wish I had protected it more with sunscreen! And as far as being "too sensitive," I now wear sensitive as a badge of honor. In words often attributed to Kristen Butler, "Sensitive people should be treasured. They love deeply and think deeply about life. They are loyal, honest, and true. The simple things sometimes mean the most to them. They don't need to change or harden. Their purity makes them who they are" (2014).

THE TAKEAWAY

Thoughts happen. We don't choose which ones arrive, nor can we control them once they appear. Sometimes it can feel as if we are puppets on a string. Our worries, beliefs, inner PEBS, and suit of armor stories are like one big thought-puppeteer. The thought-puppeteer controls all our movements—our arms, our legs, and even our mouths.

If our adventurous side says, "Jump!" and our mind says, "How high? Not high. Not high at all. We might fall and get hurt. In fact, best not jump at all," the thought-puppeteer keeps our feet on the ground, even if adventure is something we value.

To take back our movements, we need to cut the strings. The thought-puppeteer can still be hovering above, wiggling the wooden crossbars, but without connected strings the movements remain our own. The puppeteer can hold the bars still, and we can still choose to jump.

Difficult thoughts and unwanted emotional pain are what push our detonators. When we are fused with the content of thoughts and respond to emotional pain with experiential avoidance, we set off the bomb by allowing internal experiences to dictate our choices in values-incongruent ways. Mindful awareness of internal experiences expands the space between detonator and bomb; willingness and defusion neutralize it.

Chapter 8

Finding Force in a Fresh Self

We need to do a better job of putting ourselves higher on our own to-do list.

—Michelle Obama

"Tell me about yourself." We've all heard this prompt on dates, during interviews, or in psychotherapy. Take a moment to consider how you might respond if I asked you to tell me about who you are and what you are like.

Our sense of self or identity often comes in the form of a narrative we construct around our thoughts, feelings, and roles—things like I am a wife, I am a mom, I am a professional, I am a student; I am anxious, I am nice, I can't let things go, I am friendly; I am liberal, I am conservative, I am Jewish, I am an atheist; I am a dog person, I am a cat person, I am outdoorsy; and so on.

We may consider elements of the narrative to be positive (I am nice), negative (I can't let things go), or neutral (I am outdoorsy). Regardless of the perceived valence, we risk psychological inflexibility if we become fused with our narratives ("That's just who I am") and allow them to dictate our actions in the absence of guiding values.

Bring It On: Who Am I? Part I

Grab your journal and respond to the prompt "Tell me about yourself." Write down your response.

Next, in your journal, complete these statements using all the words that come to mind:

I am _____.

I am a _____.

Now, using the responses from above, complete these statements:

Being _____ means I _____.

Being _____ means _____.

Your written responses might look something like:

I am *anxious*. Being *anxious* means I *am unable to enjoy life like other people*.

I am *overweight*. Being *overweight* means *no one will ever want to date me*.

I am *a mom*. Being *a mom* means I *should always put my kids first, no matter what*.

I am *a female cop*. Being *a female cop* means I *can't show weakness*.

Reflect on your entry and what it says about your sense of self.

SELF-ISH

In ACT, the stories we construct about ourselves, our roles, and our identities are referred to as our *conceptualized self* (Hayes, Strosahl, and Wilson 1999). Overattachment to the conceptualized self occurs when we are unable to separate ourselves from our stories. We call this type of fusion *self-as-content*. Essentially it means, I *am* my thoughts, feelings, and roles. This is problematic (psychologically inflexible) when stories, rather than values, determine our choices.

Let's look once again to Sepidah from chapter 6 as an example. Her narrative would include statements like, "I am a wife and mom. Being a stay-at-home wife and mom means I am responsible for my family and the household. I am anxious and stressed. Being anxious and stressed means I am more likely to suffer physical health problems. I am kind and helpful. Being kind and helpful means I shouldn't think poorly of others and should go out of my way to ensure others' happiness and comfort. If I do so, my family and I will be less likely to suffer the bad energy that unkindness may bring, which will in turn protect us from physical health problems."

At first glance, this narrative may seem fairly benign. However, fusion with those self-statements leads to life choices that are determined by the statements, whether they are values congruent or not.

Sepidah was so concerned about stress causing health problems that she quit a job she loved and was very good at. Then, as a stay-at-home mom, she took on 100 percent of the family responsibilities, leading to an increase in stress. Noticing her high stress level led her to worry more about developing health problems, so she attempted to control the stress by taking walks and saying no to social invitations.

This led to the unwillingness paradox (she was stressed about having stress, so she was stressed) and meant sacrificing time with friends, which had been important to her. When she was unsuccessful at controlling the stress, she became overly kind and polite, and overly accommodating with her family, hoping this would protect her from bad energy and illness. This meant that she rarely set limits, stood up for herself, or asked for help, causing even more stress and anxiety, and leading her to sacrifice her values of autonomy, self-care, and self-respect.

In addition, as her children became young adults, they struggled to function independently due to her overaccommodation, giving her even more to worry about. Her overaccommodation was also not consistent with her mom values—to parent lovingly but firmly when needed.

Sepidah's inability to separate her self from her story (self-as-content: I am my thoughts, feelings, and roles) created a vicious cycle of experiential avoidance and psychological inflexibility. Her values were nowhere to be found in her chosen actions.

Bring It On: Who Am I? Part II

Return to your personal narrative. Write down answers to the following questions:

* In what ways has fusion with your conceptualized self created psychological inflexibility in your life?

* How has overidentification with your self-statements ("this is just who/how I am") led to experiential avoidance, values-inconsistent choices, or other stuckness?

* Where do you notice no-win situations arising? In other words, do statements within your story conflict and make it impossible to be who the story says you are or "should" be? For example, what occurs when faced with a home-versus-work decision if you are fused with "I am a mom; being a good mom means I should always put my kids first" and "I am a female professional; being a successful female professional means I must show up to the table, be a team player, and go above and beyond to prove myself"? Do you accept the invitation to be a keynote speaker at an event that is being held the same evening of your kid's school play? Notice what happens when you rely on the "I ams" in choosing what to do or not to do.

GAINING PERSPECTIVE

There is no need to rewrite the story or create a new and improved self—overattachment to *any* narrative will likely lead to psychological inflexibility. What is needed as an alternative to fusion with the conceptualized self—self-as-content—is to step out of the stories and adopt a more *flexible perspective*—self-as-context (Hayes, Strosahl, and Wilson 1999).

You may remember the observing self from chapter 7. The observing self is a flexible, self-as-context perspective that is the opposite of fusing with the conceptualized self. From this standpoint, you have a narrative, but you are not your narrative. You exist separate from this narrative—you are the container of it. You (a.k.a. self) are the *context* in which the *content* emerges. Shifting to this perspective creates the flexibility to experience life as it unfolds and to choose actions based on values, rather than based on stories about the self.

You might think of your observing self like the solar system, and the thoughts, feelings, and roles that make up your self-story as the planets: the solar system contains the planets but is also separate from them. The planets orbit, sometimes closer to the sun, sometimes farther away: the solar system holds all of this, plus asteroids, comets, moons, and more. The solar system is unaffected and unharmed by all these moving parts. It exists safely in the background, stable at its core, and the holder of its various elements.

Sometimes you become myopically aware of only the Earth, or you feel as if you are spinning on an axis or caught up in an orbit. But the more you can step back, adopting a perspective of self that is like the solar system, rather than the planets, the more freely you can practice acceptance and make values-driven choices.

The conceptualized self is made up of ever-changing thoughts, feelings, sensations, and roles, whereas the observing self is the stable, unchanging You that transcends those experiences. Take a moment to think back to some of the following occasions, trying to recall them in detail, seeing them from behind your eyes as you were at that time: the Columbine school shooting, 9/11, the election of President Trump.

Now recall a memory from childhood. Now recall your most recent birthday. And now become aware of what you're doing right now as you're reading this book. See if you can notice that, across time and experiences, and despite changes in your body, knowledge, thoughts, emotions, and roles, there has been a stable You that has been present, behind your eyes, seeing and experiencing the world—a You that has *held* those thoughts and stories but has also been separate from them—the You that has been you throughout your entire life (Hayes, Strosahl, and Wilson 1999).

This observer perspective creates a space from where you can safely contact uncomfortable or unwanted internal experiences. Taking an observer perspective is not intended to remove discomfort; rather, the transcendent, unchanging You need not be threatened by the content of your thoughts and feelings because its only job is to observe these things, as they are, in each moment. From this perspective, willingness can emerge, and with it the space for values-driven choices to be made. Self-as-context is another tool for deactivating the bomb.

Bring It On: Self as Anthropologist

Imagine you are an anthropologist, but instead of studying the cultural practices of Australian Aborigines, you're observing the practices that occur inside of yourself and your life—your thoughts, feelings, physical sensations, memories, and roles (Stoddard and Afari 2014). To be an effective anthropologist, you must use observational methods that allow you to gain valuable information without intruding on or impacting that which is being studied. You use an etic, or science-oriented, approach that allows you to observe separately and impartially. As the anthropologist, you don't become one with these experiences; rather, you must remain a separate observer of them.

Use your journal to take objective field notes on the internal practices you observe as they arise. As you think, observe, and write, notice who is thinking, observing, and writing.

Your entry might look something like, "The statement *I am too anxious for socializing right now* just appeared in the Mind Village. Throat Tightness and Stomach Butterflies have joined, and with them, Dread and Urge to Avoid. I am observing them interact with one another, noticing the intensity of each rise and fall."

Read your entry back to yourself, then reflect on the difference between fusion with *I am too anxious for socializing right now* and the defused anthropologist: "The statement *I am too anxious for socializing* has just appeared in the Mind Village; I am observing its presence."

THE MISSING THINK

We have talked about several forms of thinking that can lead us away from a mighty life when we become fused with their content: the inner PEBS warnings (worries), the suit of armor beliefs (schemas that develop to make sense of early experiences), and the conceptualized self ("I am my stories"). The final link in the mind chain is thinking that is dominated by the Inner Critic.

The Universal Inner Critic

I frequently have clients in my anxiety clinic who struggle with high levels of self-criticism. They hold themselves to impossibly high standards, so the voice of their Inner Critic is constantly reminding them of their inadequacies. It's a very painful space, occupied by insecurity and pressure to be and do better. Does this sound familiar?

It appears that nearly all humans share the experience of having an Inner Critic. If you are reading this and have no idea what I'm talking about ("I never have negative thoughts about myself or my worth. I always feel perfectly confident and adequate. I don't know what she's talking about."), please do let me know! To date, I have never had a client, student, supervisee, or workshop attendee raise a hand when I've asked who does not have an Inner Critic.

This universality feels pretty important. If it's the case that nearly all humans have some version of an "I'm not good enough" inner voice, how can it be that this is pathological? Remember the skunk and all that stuff about evolution from chapter 6? Based on all we know, it simply wouldn't make sense for a universal human experience to be an accident.

Think about your own Inner Critic. What does she tell you? Is it possible that, while you don't like how mean she can be, she is not here by accident? That she has a purpose? That she is, in some way, trying to protect or motivate you? Mine (I call her Sheila) tells me that I'm average and ordinary. That I'm "fine" or "okay" but certainly nothing special. She compares me to other people and points out how much better and smarter they are. Her favorite quip is that I'm a fraud, an imposter—that I don't actually have any business writing books or sharing my so-called "knowledge" (see, that was Sheila typing "so-called" and putting "knowledge" in quotes—she can be such a jerk!).

It's hard to feel the pain, inadequacy, and self-doubt that arise when Sheila shows up. *And* I see how she is trying to keep me on my toes. She is trying to motivate me to avoid complacency and to strive to better myself. She is trying to protect me from putting myself out there and being rejected or humiliated (we are social creatures who need to remain in good standing with our tribes, after all!).

Importantly, she knows what matters to me. She rarely criticizes my cooking (even though she'd be right) because being a world-class chef is not on my bucket list (or any list, for that matter). She couldn't care less about my driving or my finances. She saves her opinions for my family, my creative work, and my career. Why? *Because she wants to make sure I don't let the important stuff slide.*

Bring It On: Name That Critic

Before we move on, it's time to name your Inner Critic. You are about to start treating this part of yourself quite differently, so let's get to know her a little first.

What would you like to call your Inner Critic? Giving her a name is a form of defusion that will create some separation between you and the insults she hurls. Your critic can have a human name like mine, or you can call her "The Mouthy Teen," "Megaphone," "The Corrupt Judge," or "Roger Ebert" (the former movie critic, for those of you too young to remember). Be creative, have fun! Write her name in your journal. We will listen to her indictments (and respond in a new way) a little later in the chapter.

Our Inner Critic is *trying* to be helpful; *how* we respond to her makes all the difference. Because, as it turns out, the harder we are on ourselves the less likely we are to move forward in new ways (Kannan and Levitt 2013). What happened the last time your Inner Critic scolded you for being lazy and demanded that you exercise more? How effective was she when she chewed you out for procrastinating and commanded you, like Kanye, to work harder, better, faster, stronger?

Maybe you listened to her for a time, then rebelled. Or maybe she made you feel so bad about yourself that you just gave up and stayed stuck. The Inner Critic is commonly joined by sadness, shame, contempt, and disgust (Whelton and Greenberg 2005). When these internal experiences are met with fusion and experiential avoidance, a mighty life moves farther from our reach. *The Inner Critic rarely effects values-consistent change when we are fused with her judgments.*

The solution is not to silence the Inner Critic (not that we could—she's here to stay, just like the skunk's smelly butt), or to convince her that she's wrong (bet you've already tried to Stuart Smalley your way out of this, and yet, here you still are)—but to take a more active role in how we choose to respond when she gets insolent.

SELF-COMPASSION

Learning to practice self-compassion is a powerful form of acceptance and defusion that provides an alternative response to the Inner Critic. It also opens a path to greater psychological flexibility.

Self-compassion comprises three interconnected components (Neff 2003):

1. **Mindfulness of suffering**—nonjudgmental, present-moment awareness of the thoughts, feelings, sensations, and urges that are causing personal pain

2. **Common humanity**—seeing suffering as a universally shared experience among human beings (like the skunk and his bum!)

3. **Self-kindness**—nurturing yourself with warmth and understanding

In practice, if your Inner Critic shows up as you're reading, notice her words and become aware of how you feel physically and emotionally. Consider all the other women who are struggling with anxiety, some of whom may even be reading this book, and know we are here because we are suffering too. Our specific forms of pain may be different, but we are in this together.

Then breathe, making space for it all. Thank your Inner Critic by name for trying to protect or motivate you, for reminding you what you care about. Then summon the kindest part of yourself for an "Atta girl—way to keep going and trying—life is hard! How brave to persevere through your anxiety toward a bolder you and a mightier life." You might even name her too (my anti-Sheila is Imaginary Oprah; to summon her I think, "WWOS": what would Oprah say? Some days it's "You get compassion! You get compassion! Everybody gets compassion!").

You're not trying to change your mind by convincing yourself of how great you are. You're not minimizing or invalidating your experience of anxiety. And you're not making excuses, engaging in self-pity, being selfish, or letting yourself off the hook (self-compassion is sometimes misunderstood in this way; Orsillo and Roemer 2011).

You are observing your internal experiences and accepting them as a normal (albeit uncomfortable) part of being human, and relating with those experiences from a place of genuine kindness. Why? Because research has shown that self-compassion is associated with greater resilience (Raes 2010), optimism (Neff and Vonk 2009), feelings of social connectedness (Neff, Kirkpatrick, and Rude 2007), personal initiative, positive affect (Neff, Rude, and Kirkpatrick 2007), and a greater sense of overall well-being and life satisfaction (Neff 2003). Self-compassion even buffers against social comparison and rumination (Neff 2008).

Self-compassion can also offer a lifeline when self-esteem is low (Neff 2011). High self-esteem may bring temporary feelings of happiness (Baumeister et al. 2003), but to have high self-esteem, our Inner Critic essentially has to stay mute. And who are we kidding? Talk about Mission Impossible.

Self-esteem is not all it's cracked up to be. It fluctuates constantly depending on our current inner state-of-my-perceived-self-worth address. To have high self-esteem, we have to believe we are special, that we are better than everyone else, and this often means putting others down so we might salvage our own self-esteem (Neff 2011). Yuck!

But self-compassion is different. It is a way of relating to ourselves, in any given moment—whether we like or dislike ourselves or our circumstances—that promotes self-awareness (mindfulness of our suffering) and self-kindness, without the need to disparage others (common humanity). So forget trying to improve your self-esteem, and start practicing self-compassion.

What if you were to treat yourself as kindly as you treat the ones you love? Can you imagine it? Right now, bring to mind someone you love fiercely. Imagine holding this person's (or pet's) face in your hands, cupping it gently, bringing it up close to your own, and giving it a "nosey nosey" (what my mom used to say when I was little and she would gently rub her nose against mine). Look right into those eyes you love, that face, and feel how completely you adore this being. If you knew your loved one was in pain, that her Inner Critic had convinced her she had no worth, what would you do? What would you offer?

Now pull back a few inches and imagine the face you are cradling in your hands is your own at around age five or six. Can you offer her the same tender love, support, and compassion? Now bring that little you into your adult body. Can you even offer *her* that loving-kindness?

Clear and Murky Pain

You know kindness and compassion. If that loved one or a baby or a puppy was hurt and in pain, you wouldn't shake it, yell at it, or smack it upside the head. You wouldn't roll your eyes and scoff with "Just get over it, you big baby." And yet, this is exactly what we do to ourselves in our own minds. We go to war with ourselves—and that can't possibly end well. What will become of the loser? Or the winner? There simply can't be a winner.

Life hurts, especially in the places that matter to us most. For example, if you long to be included by a group, but fail to receive an invitation to their event, of course you will feel hurt and disappointed. This is *clear pain*. It's natural hurt you feel in response to a connected problem (Hayes, Strosahl, and Wilson 2012). Other examples of clear pain might be anger when you have been wronged, guilt when you have done wrong, or grief when you have experienced a loss. Of note, *grief* can involve a vast array of emotions, all of which would be considered normal and natural reactions to loss; thus, grief, when you experience loss, is clear pain.

Often, however, clear pain is accompanied by *murky pain*, or layers of added emotion that spring from trying to resist the clear stuff (Hayes, Strosahl, and Wilson 2012). For example, if your mother criticizes your appearance, you might feel hurt. This is clear pain. If you try to avoid the hurt, but are not successful, this may result in you feeling angry with yourself or even ashamed for "letting" yourself feel hurt;

the anger and shame are murky pain. You might think of clear pain as the natural reaction, and murky pain as the reaction to the reaction. Murky pain is one of the many costs of experiential avoidance.

But imagine the difference if you were to respond to your clear pain with self-compassion instead. You would be able to (1) notice your clear pain (becoming aware of the hurt in response to your mom's criticism), (2) remember that you are not alone in your very human suffering (perhaps remembering other women who struggle with critical family members), and (3) offer yourself kindness and care because you are hurting (*Of course it hurts*, *This is hard*, *You are more than your appearance*). Self-compassion won't take away the hurt, but it will prevent the anger and shame from getting layered on top of it.

Bring It On: Compassionate Hero

Let's continue to practice self-kindness by inviting a wise, compassionate, and mighty superhero to join us for a bit (Scarlet 2018). All superheroes, like Wonder Woman and Black Widow, have an origin story: how they acquired their powers and why they decided to fight for justice. Often, their stories involve pain, loss, trauma, and a moment of deciding to change.

Each of us has our own unique origin story. Take a few moments to consider yours. In your journal, reflect on a defining moment (or series of moments) that has shaped you. Perhaps a great loss, a highly critical parent, childhood abuse or neglect, or a traumatic event (e.g., rape, assault, accident, combat, disaster). Take some time to consider your origin story and write it down (you can use the suit of armor exercise you completed in chapter 6, if you'd like). Talk about the experiences that may have contributed to your struggle with anxiety or that may have given rise to the voice of your Inner Critic.

Now take a few moments to identify a personal superhero. This is someone you look up to; someone you see as a figure of ultimate wisdom and compassion. This could be a real person, such as a grandparent, a therapist, a star athlete, or a historical figure (e.g.,

Oprah Winfrey, Helen Keller, Christine Blasey Ford). Or it can be a fictional character, such as Batgirl, Katniss Everdeen, or Minerva McGonagall. Think of the qualities you admire in your superhero and write them down.

Now take a few moments to imagine that you have some alone time together. Your superhero knows exactly what you have been through, what your origin story is, and how it has shaped you (because she or he has been there too!). Your hero is understanding, supportive, warm, caring, and encouraging. She or he has risen above the origin story and knows you can too. She or he knows exactly what to say to you and what you need to hear.

What would your superhero say to you? How might she or he express awareness of your suffering, a sense of common humanity, and kindness? Take a few moments to write it down.

What happens to us—our pain, our trauma history, our struggles with anxiety, stress, worry, fear, and self-doubt—does not define us. These things are merely a part of our origin story and are not our fault. Now it is up to us to decide whether we want to answer the hero's call and how we will choose to continue the rest of our hero's journey.

Take the voice of your compassionate hero with you. When your Inner Critic shows up, bring your Compassionate Hero into the conversation. Allow your Hero to encourage you to move in directions that fit with your deeply held personal values.

Gosh Darn It, People Like Me

It feels important to clarify that self-kindness does not mean we simply say nice things to ourselves in an effort to feel better. First, self-compassion is not something we practice to *remove* the hurt; it is something we practice *because* we hurt. The word "compassion" comes from the Latin "to suffer with" (Tirch, Schoendorff, and Silberstein 2014). If your friend is grieving the loss of her mother, you might offer a warm hug and words of loving-kindness: "I'm so sorry you have to go through this. I'm here." Unless you possess magical healing powers, I imagine you hold no illusions that your kind words are going to take away her grief. And yet, you offer support when you see her in pain. You suffer with. Self-kindness works the same way: "It's really hard to go through this. I'm here."

Positive self-statements *can* be consistent with self-compassion as a form of self-kindness: "I believe in you. You've persevered through so much." In many cases, though, affirmations—"I'm good enough, I'm smart enough, and gosh darn it, people like me"—can backfire and make you feel even worse (especially if you have low self-esteem; Wood, Perunovic, and Lee 2009).

If your Inner Critic tells you, for example, that you are not interesting enough, thin enough, or organized enough, and your Inner Obnoxious Cheerleader responds with "I am fascinating! I am gorgeous! I've got my life in perfect order!" what do you notice? Try it right now with a negative belief you hold about yourself. Does blowing that sunshine feel truly kind? Does it respect your suffering? Or does it invalidate your pain and suggest you are supposed to think and feel differently, which then adds layers of murky pain?

The problem with affirmations is that they have to be believed to feel kind. And if you believed them, you wouldn't need them! Affirmations, and positive self-talk in general, are often just fusion and avoidance in disguise.

Bring It On: Compassionate Conversation

In your journal, label the tops of three separate pages: "Inner Critic" (you can use the specific name you created), "Me," and "Compassionate Me." Then, using the second-person point of view, follow the steps below (Kolts 2016), completing each one before moving on to the next:

1. On the Inner Critic page: Write down the things your Inner Critic typically says to you.

2. On the Me page: Respond to the Inner Critic by telling her how she makes you feel and in what ways her abuse impacts you (is she helpful or hurtful?).

3. On the Inner Critic page: Respond to Me by explaining what it is that you want for her and why it is that you are so hard on her. Let her know what it is that you are trying to do for her—how you are trying to help or motivate her. Explain what you are afraid might happen should you go silent.

4. On the Me page: Respond to the Inner Critic by acknowledging her efforts, maybe identifying early hurts that gave birth to her, as a way to show understanding and empathy for her. Then let the Inner Critic know what you really need. How might she be helpful to you in a different way?

5. Now take a moment to slow down. Take three mindful breaths.

6. On the Compassionate Me page: From a place of wisdom and kindness, summarize what you have come to understand about yourself. Then respond to the Inner Critic and Me by acknowledging their suffering (mindfulness), telling them that they are not alone (common humanity), and offering words of loving-kindness.

If the Inner Critic is the devil who sits on one shoulder, dust off some space on your other to make room for your Compassionate Me.

THE TAKEAWAY

Our sense of self often comes from "I am" statements we construct about our roles and experiences (internal and external). Fusion with this *conceptualized self*, or self-as-content, is problematic (psychologically inflexible) when our narratives (including our Inner Critic) rather than our values determine our choices. When fusion with self-stories presses the detonator, harnessing your observing (self-as-context) and compassionate self is your final tool for deactivating the bomb by seeing your stories as separate from yourself, remembering common humanity, and focusing on self-kindness.

Chapter 9

Charging Toward Your Best You

You can't be that kid standing at the top of the waterslide, overthinking it. You have to go down the chute.

—Tina Fey

They say, "Knowledge is power," and after eight chapters, hopefully you have a good amount of powerful new information. But knowledge only takes you so far. Reading this book is a fierce first step toward building psychological flexibility in service of having a mighty life. But reading books didn't win Serena her twenty-three Grand Slam championships, nor did it make Danica Patrick the most successful woman in the history of automobile racing. At some point, you have to pick up the racket and get behind the wheel (but not at the same time).

In ACT, we call this *committed action* (Hayes, Strosahl, and Wilson 1999). Of course, committing to new action can be difficult and daunting, especially if you've grown accustomed to feeling competent in your comfort zone. I will admit (and if I didn't, my husband would be happy to admit it for me!) that I don't like things I'm not good at. I'm not proud of that, but thankfully, I have my values to help me stick with the stuff that matters, whether I'm good at it or not. And typically, with some practice, "not so good at" becomes "better at," as larger patterns of committed action are built.

So it's time to shimmy into that black catsuit, pick up the racket, charge the net, and hit the snot out of some balls. As you do, remember two key things:

1. Serena still loses some matches—because progress is never linear, and

2. Serena still takes tennis lessons—because growth is lifelong, and sometimes we need outside guidance.

Hopefully you have already been giving some new things a try: using mindfulness as a vehicle for curiously and impartially observing your myriad thoughts, and willingly expanding to allow emotions and sensations to accompany you in this one moment (and the next, and the next).

As you sharpen your powers of mindful awareness, thought defusion (including self-as-context), and emotional acceptance, you will cultivate an optimal context for consciously choosing values-driven action and charging toward your best you. Of course, sometimes the hard stuff gets in the way. What have your roadblocks been so far?

I WILL WHEN

Maybe you have found yourself thinking, *Yeah, this psychological flexibility stuff sounds great, I'm all in! As soon as _____ happens/changes/improves.* I call this the "I will when" trap. Look at your experience and see if you can find "I will when" hiding in the corners of your stuck places. "**I will** start dating **when** I lose twenty pounds," "**I will** apply for the promotion **once** I feel confident I can get it," "**I'll** tell my partner how I feel **as soon as** I feel a little more secure about her feelings for me."

I'Wyl Wen is a powerful supervillain. She can shape-shift into other forms like Ikant Un'Tyl and Ayum-Jst WeytingForr. She says things like, "**I can't** wear my sexy lingerie **until** I get my pre-baby body back" and "**I'm just waiting for** the right time to ask my supervisor for a raise." She uses her powers of mind control to manipulate those under her spell into believing she is "a good reason." And she secretly pours slow-drying cement around her victims' feet, making forward motion seem utterly impossible.

And, in a way, this makes perfect sense. Let's look at the logical next sentence: "Because if I _____ now, before _____, then _____ might happen." "**Because if I** start dating/apply for the promotion/tell my partner how I feel **before** I lose weight/know I can get it/feel secure, **then** I will be rejected/humiliated/hurt."

I'Wyl Wen is using more sticky language in disguise—or maybe not so in disguise! Do you remember learning that only we humans are capable of worrying about *just about anything*, even if we have never directly experienced that thing? This is because we learn at a very young age to relate objects to one another in ways that create a vast web of learned relationships, regardless of experience (Hayes, Barnes-Holmes, and Roche 2001).

Let's look at an example. Let's say I tell you that this right here ℘ is my friend Mookie, and this ♠ is a bleezle. ℘ hates bleezles because bleezles love morgenberries. How do you think Mookie feels about morgenberries? Before you answer, let's look at all the connections, or relations, your brain can make between symbols and words (which, of course, are also symbols).

Here is what I told you directly:

℘ = Mookie

♠ = bleezle

℘ hates bleezles

Bleezles love morgenberries

Now look at the relations you can *derive* from that information without having any direct experience or knowledge. In other words, these are things I did not tell you directly but that your brain can figure out on its own.

Mookie hates bleezles.

Mookie hates ♠.

℘ hates ✿.

✿ loves morgenberries.

Now let's go back to the question of how you think Mookie feels about morgenberries. You might think that Mookie hates morgenberries because (1) you have derived that Mookie hates bleezles, and (2) we know this is because bleezles love morgenberries, so you (3) derive that Mookie must hate morgenberries. Sort of like the expression "The friend (morgenberries) of my enemy (bleezles) is my enemy (morgenberries) too."

Or you might differently derive that Mookie loves morgenberries because you derived this too:

Morgenberries contains "berries."

Berries are food.

Food is eaten.

Food that is eaten has a finite supply.

Morgenberries are food.

Morgenberries are eaten.

Morgenberries have a finite supply.

Bleezles/✿ eat morgenberries.

Therefore because (1) bleezles love morgenberries, and (2) morgenberries are foods that are eaten, (3) bleezles might eat all the morgenberries, taking them away from Mookie. In this case, the friend (bleezles) of my friend (morgenberries) is my enemy (bleezles). Wow, that's a vast relational network! And it all came from these two simple little sentences: ℘ is my friend Mookie, and this ✿ is a bleezle. ℘ hates bleezles because bleezles love morgenberries.

Humans can relate objects in a variety of ways—better/worse, louder/softer, here/there, if/then, near/far, same/different—and while this ability is exactly what allows us to solve abstract problems, it is also what allows us to feel fear in the absence of danger (Hayes, Barnes-Holmes, and Roche 2001).

So what does all this have to do with I'Wyl Wen? Through the same process, you draw conclusions in the absence of direct knowledge or experience *all the time* and those conclusions come with painful feelings. Your complex web of relations ("Small bodies *are better than* bigger bodies, having a bigger body *causes* rejection, *if* I date while bigger, *then* I will be rejected, being rejected *is the same* as being worthless," and so on) leads to the conclusion that it's not a good idea to date before you lose twenty pounds. And it comes with a heap of anxiety and fear, even if you haven't experienced overt rejection due to your weight.

Having Is Not Believing

So now what? How can a Mighty Heroine rescue herself from this sneaky I'Wyl Wen supervillain?

First, you begin by noticing her presence ("Aha, I've spotted you, 'I will share my feelings, as soon as I feel comfortable!'"). Second, you remember that *having thoughts* is not the same as *believing their content* as Gospel Truth or doing as they command.

If I'Wyl Wen says, "Jump!" you have a near infinite number of behavioral options: (1) jump, (2) do nothing, (3) ask, "How high?", (4) spin around in circles, (5) choose any other movement, (6) strap springs on your feet, and so on. You can autopilot jump when your mind says jump (and notice how this typically leads to unworkable action), or you can notice the thought, connect with your values, and consider whether following the thought as Gospel Truth will be in line with the Me you want to be and the life you want to live. If it will, absolutely do as it says. If it won't, think one way but act another. Let's try it.

Bring It On: Think One Way, Act Another

Let's play a quick game of I'Wyl Wen Says. It's exactly the same as Simon Says from when you were a kid, only this time you are going to harness your Inner Rebel and break all the rules. Or not. You get to choose.

For the following prompts that begin with "I'Wyl Wen says," choose to follow some but not others. For the prompts that do not begin with "I'Wyl Wen says," do the same. You can do nothing as a way to not respond, or you can choose to do something that is different from that of the prompt. Ready?

* I'Wyl Wen says wave your right hand.

* I'Wyl Wen says nod your head.

* Tap your toes.

* I'Wyl Wen says tap your toes.

* Shake your head back and forth.

* Wink your left eye.

* I'Wyl Wen says give a little whistle.

So now we know you have the ability to *choose* to do or not do what your mind says (it was your mind reading those prompts, after all). This is a form of defusion. You are observing your thoughts, remaining unhooked from their content, and making a conscious choice about how to respond. Of course, eye winks and toe taps are easier than dates and promotions because they don't come with the fear (unless you super care about your winking and toe-tapping abilities, that is). But, at a basic level, we now know you have the ability to think one way and act another. If you are willing to feel the feelings so you can have the life you want, then the Mighty Heroine will defeat the Evil Supervillain. So, Mighty Heroine:

1. Turn on your X-ray vision and illuminate those sticky thoughts and difficult feelings.

2. Tie on your Cape of Commitment (and stand arms akimbo!).

3. Summon your squad: Defusion Girl, Willingness Woman, Self-Compassion Sister.

4. Boldly declare, "I've got you now, I'Wyl Wen—my X-ray vision grants me the might of mindfulness, and I have spotted your relational web of evil tricks: 'I Can't Untils' and 'Once I do this, then I'll do thats'! Your cement is no match for my force of flexibility!"

5. Fly in the direction of your values.

I don't mean to suggest that flying forward is *easy*. There are no simple answers or quick fixes for committed action (if there were, I promise I'd be sharing them!). Stepping out of your Comfort Zone and into your Courage Zone *necessarily* means trading ease for feelings of vulnerability. It's like coming to a fork in the road where you must choose one option: Take the road to the right that you always travel—it is well worn and familiar, an easy terrain to navigate, but will lead to the same place it always has; you get comfort but trade possibility. Take the road to the left that you have never taken—this one appears winding, hilly, and flanked on all sides by strange and exotic flora; you can't know for sure how that journey will go or where the road will lead; you have to feel vulnerable but open to possibility. Or stand at the fork forever. Not choosing is still choosing. You avoid vulnerability but stay stuck moving nowhere. When you stand at that crossroads, who is the Me you want to be?

The ACT processes you've been trying on are just that: processes. There are no final destinations—a Mighty Heroine's work is never done. But maybe the Mighty Heroine (that's you, by the way) who defeats I'Wyl Wen is Lava Lady—Lava doesn't need obstacles to be removed in order to keep flowing forward. She burns through weak ones, flows around stronger ones, and even picks up and carries a few along with her, all the while flowing forward. Lava Lady is a force to be reckoned with.

Bring It On: Volcanic Lair Plan

Alright, Lava Lady, let's use your volcanic lair to make a plan for committed action (you can also see a graphic depiction of the Volcanic Lair Plan at http://www.newharbinger.com/34413).

Let's start by identifying a *life domain* that is especially important to you. Life domains include things like friendship, family (parenting, family of origin, extended family), romantic relationships, career, service/community/activism, spirituality/religion, culture, education/development, finances, recreation, and health/well-being (Hayes, Strosahl, and Wilson 2012). In your journal, it might be helpful to rank these, or just highlight your top three. Then *choose one* to begin your Volcanic Lair Plan.

If you're feeling feisty, draw a volcano with three layers. Your domain goes at the narrow top of your volcano.

Next, let's take the elevator down to the middle of the lair and identify some values—qualities of being and doing—that represent the Me you want to be as you engage within the domain of living you have chosen. So, for example, if you picked friendship as your domain, you might choose authentic, caring, and adventurous as values. (You can always revisit the worksheet The Me I Want to Be, at http://www.newharbinger.com/34413, for a list of values words.) For this middle layer, choose two to four qualities.

Finally, let's dive into the belly of the beast and identify some committed actions that represent specific, doing-what-matters, workable actions that are in line with the values above, all within the chosen domain. Here, be sure to stick with things you can control: your voice, your hands, and your feet. Returning to the friendship example, these might be things like "Call bestie and share about relationship challenge" (in service of being authentic), "Send BFF card for no reason" (in service of being caring), "Accept social invitation to indoor skydiving" (in service of being adventurous).

Notice what shows up as you write. What emotions, worries, or doubts emerge that threaten to become obstacles? For whom are you willing to make up the lair guest room? Write these all around your volcano.

Now, let your volcano erupt, Lava Girl! Flow authentically while you share yourself with your bestie! Burn through your fear while adventurously blowing around with your pals! Repeat this (domain, values, actions, potential obstacles), now or later, for any other important life domain you wish to make a priority in your volcanic lair plan.

EXTERNAL OBSTACLES

Any number of challenges can present as potential obstacles to committed action. So far, we've been focusing on difficult internal experiences that have formerly compelled us in unworkable ways. But external obstacles—such as time, money, pushback from others, or access to resources—can certainly act as obstacles as well.

Pop quiz: when obstacles occur, can we (A) rely on language to produce "good reasons" for why we must stop moving forward; (B) practice self-compassion by noticing our pain, recognizing we're not alone, and kindly saying to ourselves, "Oh well, you tried, but it's just not in the cards"; or (C) get creative and find a workable alternative? If you chose C, you get an A! Obstacles can be discouraging; *and* they don't have to be obstacles to charging toward your best you at all!

Many years ago, I had a client in an ACT group for veterans with chronic pain. He was a former basketball player who had sustained a serious injury that resulted in paralysis from the chest down. For him, his lack of mobility presented a pretty significant external obstacle to many of the committed actions he desired to engage in. What he wanted more than anything was to play ball again, but that simply wasn't possible. So we got creative.

We explored all the facets of basketball that felt meaningful to him (was it competition, strategizing, being part of a team, being physically active?). By the end of our time together, he had gone from spending most of his time at home, alone, in his wheelchair, despairing and longing for a very different life, to being a popular basketball coach. Importantly, this didn't erase his pain (physical or emotional). In fact, he had to reduce his dose of narcotic pain medication to be able to think more clearly, so his physical pain got a bit worse. And sitting on the sidelines watching others do on the court what he was no longer able to was quite emotionally painful for him. But neither was as painful as sitting home doing nothing with nobody. And he got his groove back by being on that court.

Obstacles Incognito

Sometimes external obstacles are really unwanted internal experiences in disguise. For example, I have always had a tough time with exercise. It's just never been something I've loved, and I've always found it difficult to follow through with exercise-related committed actions. And wow, let me tell you, I sure did have a *lot* of "external obstacles" to blame: I don't have time, it's too dark, it's too sunny, it's too late, it's too early, it's too hot, it's too cold, I need new sneakers, there's no one chasing me—the list goes on and on. But truth be told, the real obstacle was my *apathy*—I just wasn't into it.

When something really matters, true obstacles have creative workarounds. In my case, my thoughts (like *I don't have time*) and feelings (like apathy) acted as obstacles, and they were difficult to circumvent because I wasn't in touch with any part of exercise that *truly* mattered to me. Exercise felt like something I *should* do, not something I was freely choosing from a place of values.

Then one day, my aha moment arrived. I was sitting on the sofa with my hubby. He is one of those lucky dudes who eats what he wants and looks like he works out (I have a love-hate relationship with this part of him—love to look at him, jealous as all get-out that his physique comes so effortlessly). In reality, he is almost entirely sedentary. This was the moment exercise *truly* began to matter to me: I thought,

My kids can't grow up with two sedentary parents. I realized that modeling physical activity for my kids was the missing piece of my values puzzle.

Don't get me wrong, I didn't start going to the gym every day at five a.m. and entering bodybuilding competitions. But I did start walking, jogging, and doing yoga more regularly. I still don't love to exercise, and my mind still gives me "good reasons" why I shouldn't. And sometimes I let those reasons sway me, because at the end of the day, we are all still imperfect humans. But with a little self-compassion and a lot of reconnection to my values (sprinkled with willingness and defusion as needed), I return to it each time.

Bring It On: Obstacles Shmobstacles

In your journal:

* Jot down a committed action, either from the Volcanic Lair Plan you have already completed or one you think you might wish to work on.

* Jot down any *external* obstacles you have encountered, or imagine some you are likely to encounter, as you consider this committed action.

* Notice when external obstacles are really unwanted internal experiences in disguise (these will often appear as excuses, reasons, rationalizations, and justifications).

* Keep your why close by: reconnect with the values that are guiding your desire to engage in this committed action. Importantly, stuckness may show up if you are connecting with the "wrong" value. What I mean is, your value needs to be truly, deeply important to you personally—it's not something you think you "should" prioritize.

* Brainstorm creative work-arounds (if you are stuck, skip to the example below for guidance).

* Notice "yeah, but" thoughts that arise as you generate your work-arounds, then reconnect with your values and recommit to finding that work-around.

* Notice other thoughts, like "It doesn't count," that emerge when a work-around doesn't fit the original committed action plan. Fusion with "It doesn't count" or "It isn't the same" or "It isn't good enough" will lead to unworkable action.

For example, maybe your committed action involves going back to school for an MFA in creative arts. The obstacle is that you can't afford the tuition for the only local program. The valued domain is education and development. The values are skillfulness, creativity, and challenge. Creative work-arounds might be finding another program, even if it means commuting or moving. If that's not possible because of family obligations (or other true external obstacles), perhaps you opt for an online MFA. If that is still too expensive, perhaps you forgo the MFA altogether and find a free, local art meet-up group where you can learn from peers and participate in critiques with them. In this way, you might also discover other inexpensive resources for skill-building workshops, portfolio contests, educational podcasts, the social media profiles of artists you like, and so on.

When values are your guide, the specific actions become somewhat less important. There are usually a number of ways to honor your values, as long as you are willing to get creative and hold your original plans (and desired outcomes—as we discussed in chapter 5) lightly.

Problem Solving

What we're really talking about here is some basic problem solving (D'Zurilla and Nezu 2006). So how can you be a Mighty COPER when you run into a barrier to committed action or into any other life problem or dilemma that needs to be addressed? Use the following guide to help you work out and evaluate your options for overcoming external obstacles (and write it down, rather than playing mental ping-pong!).

Bring It On: Mighty COPER

In your journal, work out the following (or download the Mighty COPER worksheet at http://www.newharbinger.com/34413):

* **C**omplication: Name the problem to be solved or obstacle to overcome.

* **O**ptions: Brainstorm creative options or alternatives.

* **P**ick one: Choose an option and try it out.

* **E**valuate: Evaluate how it went.

* **R**epeat: Choose a new option if needed.

Example:

* **C**omplication: *fighting with my partner constantly*

* **O**ptions: *break up, do nothing, communicate, couples counseling*

* **P**ick one: *communicate*

* **E**valuate: *helped at first, then back to square one*

* **R**epeat: *try couples counseling next, and reevaluate in six months*

As you navigate your life and its many challenges—including the problems that need solving—your self-stories, worries, Inner Critic, suit of armor beliefs, and their corresponding emotions, sensations, and urges will continue to be triggered. No therapy or skill you read about in this book or in any other will magically stop difficult internal experiences from popping in uninvited, like annoying nosey neighbors. Just remember, the thoughts and feelings are not problems in and of themselves. Uncomfortable, sure. But how we respond to their uninvited pop-ins (with psychological flexibility versus inflexibility) is what determines a mighty life.

HOLDING PLANS LIGHTLY

The A-Team's Hannibal Smith and I both love it when a plan comes together. But if there's one thing obstacles tell us about plans—wait, make that three things obstacles tell us about plans—they need to be:

1. held lightly,

2. applied flexibly, and

3. not used as a substitute for *in this one moment* valued choosing.

In other words, don't let your plan make you lose sight of your one and only true goal: building greater psychological flexibility. Nearly every moment of every day provides an opportunity to choose to show up, fully and openly, and be the Me you want to be. A plan provides a nice road map for getting started on a new and unfamiliar journey. But if you lose your Thomas Guide (old-school bound paper maps that existed before GPS—if you don't believe me, you could probably find one in the Museum of Ancient History) or encounter a downed tree or missing bridge, *you still have everything you need to continue your journey.*

What's more, we've spent a lot of time talking about the power of presence, so it may seem confusing to now be talking about plans—plans, by their very definition, are future focused. There's nothing inherently "bad" about making future-oriented plans. But when they fall apart, we need to carry on. For example, how many times have you "committed" to a New Year's resolution, or restarting some other commitment again on Monday, only to fail? And then fail again? So for our purposes, your Volcanic Lair Plan is more like a set of ideas to provide guidance—the real committed action comes in the Me you choose to be in this one moment. Then the next. And the one after that, once it arrives.

Bring It On: The Lighthouse

Let's take a minute for a metaphor that will help bring together some of the concepts we've discussed in a way that will connect the dots on the page to your own personal experience.

Imagine you are a ship sailing along on a journey of a lifetime, tacking in directions you care about, perhaps navigating toward an important destination. Suddenly, you find yourself shrouded in thick fog, no longer able to see where you are headed. Afraid you might collide with another ship or crash onto a jagged jetty, you decide to drop anchor and wait for the fog to clear. You wait and wait, but it appears the fog is here to stay. How long will you stay anchored, lifetime journey interrupted?

Luckily, there is a way to sail on, even if the fog never clears. The lighthouse. The lighthouse will bestow the gift of light, a bright beacon, illuminating a sea lane through the fog so that you can weigh anchor and get back underway, no matter how thick the fog.

In your journal, reflect on your dropped anchor:

* What obstacles make up your fog ("I will when" statements, and other thoughts, feelings, urges, sensations)?

* How long have you been waiting to move forward? Be clear—has it been months or years?

* In what ways has your anchor weighed you down, causing you to miss out on all that you deeply long for?

* How has dropping anchor kept you from discovering the magic you might find if you were to continue your journey?

* Discuss how your values might illuminate your sea lane, so that you can keep sailing toward the life you want, no matter how slowly, even when anxiety, worry, doubt, and fear envelop you. Can you look to the light as your rescue from the anchor?

THE TAKEAWAY

Committed action is walking the talk. When external obstacles arise, you can reconnect with values and find creative ways to generate workable alternatives. When internal obstacles arise, summon the might of mindfulness and call in your squad: Defusion Girl, Willingness Woman, and Self-Compassion Sister to defeat the supervillain I'Wyl Wen and her cement mixer of reasons, rationalizations, and justifications.

Chapter 10

Living Fierce: The Finale

There are two powers in the world; one is the sword and the other is the pen. There is a third power stronger than both, that of women.

—Malala Yousafzai

You made it! Nine chapters down, one to go. This final chapter will provide a summary of what you've learned so far and bring those concepts to life through the personal stories of five fierce women who have grown mightier through ACT.

My hope is that these intimate accounts of growth, vulnerability, and strength will inspire you to keep on keeping on with your own ACT journey. And to that end, you will also find specific suggestions for how you can continue to practice and apply the mighty-making components of ACT.

If you have made it this far, please know that I feel deeply honored that you have trusted me to be part of your journey, and I truly hope you have found your reading (and experiencing) valuable.

AVOIDANCE, ACCEPTANCE, AND PSYCHOLOGICAL FLEXIBILITY

We were scared, but our fear was not as strong as our courage.

—Malala Yousafzai

Emotional and physical pain can be useful sources of information, especially insofar as they highlight what we care about and compel us to act in values-consistent ways. Anxiety about our loved ones' well-being means we care about the important people in our lives, and anxiety motivates us to care for them.

However, when internal experiences are intense and uncomfortable, we often seek to avoid, escape, or control them. The strategies we use—situational or interpersonal avoidance, procrastination, and abuse of substances—"work" in the short term to give us some relief. Long term, however, the strategies keep us stuck. They don't "fix" the discomfort in any enduring way and typically move us farther from the lives we want. What we resist persists, and resistance causes suffering. To be human is to know pain—that is a given. But the suffering that comes from resisting the pain is optional.

As an alternative to resistance, we can opt for acceptance. We can allow whatever happens to already be present inside our skin to just be. We may not like or want it, *and* we can open up and allow it some space, nonetheless. When we do so, in the service of doing what matters most deeply to us, we are being psychologically flexible. Psychological flexibility has shown to be a strong predictor of human well-being, and developing it is the ultimate goal of ACT.

Now let's read a story about the power of willingness as an alternative to avoidance.

Sarah's Story

When I went to my first ACT training, I hid in the back, as I had in the classroom, hoping to never be called on, asked a question,

*or be seen. The thought of being in the spotlight was terrifying
at times.*

*Over the years of applying ACT personally, this has
thankfully changed. I began attending other workshops and
conferences, and I distinctly remember walking into a workshop
led by two amazing female ACT trainers and saying to myself,
Sit at the front—be brave.*

*Nine years later, I continue with that bravery as my
companion. In the last eighteen months, since joining a professional
women's group, there has been a significant rise in my willingness
to ask questions, speak out, and be visible. I have done things that
I never would have considered doing ten years ago. ACT has been
central to that personally and professionally, with the women in
my community playing a pivotal role. I have deep gratitude for the
learning, friendships, and community I have encountered on this
journey so far.*

Ongoing Willingness Practices

To continue your practice with willingness, try some of the
following:

- **Cross and recross your hands.** First, cross your hands
  their natural way. Notice the experience, allowing it to be
  as it is. Second, cross them the funny-feeling way. Observe
  the sensations and practice opening and allowing. Repeat
  with sitting cross-legged, first the natural-feeling way,
  then the funny-feeling way. Simply observe and allow,
  without doing anything to resist or escape. Importantly,
  pay particular attention to the urge to return to the natural-feeling way. Notice that you can feel the urge, and
  choose not to give in.

- **Wear your jewelry on the wrong hand.** Notice the
  feeling of your watch, bracelet, or rings however you typically wear them. Then switch—put your watch on your

right hand if you typically wear it on your left, and so on. Notice how this feels. Resist the urge to wiggle and fidget. Notice the desire to switch back, and just let things be. The longer you do this, notice how at some point you probably stop noticing.

- **Practice routines in an unnatural order.** Most things you do on a regular basis are likely to have a sort of ritual to them. For example, when you dress, you likely put the same leg in the same pantleg first, every time. When you brush your teeth, the order of top, bottom, left, and right is probably the same each time you brush. Notice your rituals and routines, then switch them up. If you usually shampoo before you wash your body, flip the order. Notice the feeling of being off, odd, or awkward, and open and allow this to be present, without doing anything to change or escape the discomfort.

- **Play BeanBoozled.** This is a game whereby jellybeans that are identical in appearance have two possible flavors: a typical jellybean flavor and a disgusting flavor. For example, a light green bean could be either "juicy pear" or "cut grass"; a white-and-yellow speckled bean might be "buttered popcorn" or "spoiled milk." See if you can practice mindfully observing the flavor, and practicing a willingness to experience the unpleasant flavors in an open way. Let go of facial grimaces or other forms of bracing against the taste experience. Remember, no matter the flavor, the jellybeans are all candies made from the same ingredients, so this is a safe practice for relating to an unpleasant internal experience in a new way.

- **Watch a scary movie.** Keep your eyes open. Breathe. When a jump scare occurs, notice the experience in your body—racing heart, quickened breathing—and allow your physical sensations and emotions fully and without defense. Remember—this is a fictional movie—so this is a safe practice for relating to an intense emotional and physical experience in a new way.

- **Watch sad video clips.** Go to YouTube and look for clips from sad movies (*Marley and Me, Beaches, Terms of Endearment*—okay, I know I'm dating myself with these, but I haven't watched a lot of nonanimated movies since I had kids. If you're younger and more hip than me, watch the sad stuff from this century. If you want a sad kid film, try *Up* or *Dumbo*). As you watch, connect with and open to your experience. Notice any desire to tamp down your emotions or stop yourself from crying, and see if you can let go and just feel.

- **Ride a roller coaster or other thrilling ride.** Keep your eyes open. Try putting your hands in the air. See if you can make contact with the internal experiences in an open and expansive way. Remember, this is a ninety-second recreational experience, so this is a safe practice for relating to your thoughts and feelings in a new way.

VALUES, COMMITTED ACTION, AND BARRIERS

Tell me, what is it you plan to do with your one wild and precious life?

—Mary Oliver

Values are the heart of being mighty—the Me you want to be. They are where we care, what deeply matters to us, and what we want to stand for. If values are the trail map and compass, committed actions are the steps we physically take with our feet along the hiking path.

Committed actions are what we do; values are how we do it. Whether big life moves—such as choosing to divorce or get an advanced degree—or smaller, *in this one moment*, moves—like really listening to your partner instead of waiting to speak, or taking the stairs instead of the elevator—engagement in valued living brings greater meaning, vibrance, and might.

Valued living also brings pain *because* it's where we care. If you didn't care about what your audience of colleagues thought of you, you wouldn't be nervous to share your presentation with them. But if having a voice, courage, or knowledge dissemination matter to you, maybe the juice can be worth the squeeze.

The fear and self-doubt and catastrophic predictions that arise can become barriers to committed action if we get hooked by the thoughts and retreat back into experiential avoidance. So we return to our ACT processes again and again in service of choosing values-driven actions.

Now let's hear from one woman about the power of values and commitment in the face of internal barriers.

Bridget's Story

Throughout my life, I have been terrified of not meeting expectations. More often than not, this led me to avoiding doing anything I may not be good at and frantically overpreparing for things.

When I started graduate school, learning ACT provided for me a freedom to choose actions based on what matters most to me rather than what I believed was expected of me. I have had to make space for the fear and self-doubt I carry along the way, but I have learned that discomfort gives me valuable information about what is most meaningful in my life. I use this to flexibly guide me in choosing valued actions, and I have found that the intention and quality of my actions are much better measures of success than outcomes or opinions of others.

Now I am pursuing a career I am extremely passionate about,
one in which I get to witness the inherent courage and wisdom of
humans every day.

Ongoing Values-Driven Committed Action Practices

To continue your practice with values-driven committed action, try some of the following:

- **Set a daily intention.** Choose a week during which you wake up each morning and set a different intention for that day. The intention is an important personal value you will choose to embody in whatever ways emerge throughout the day. So you might wake up Monday, setting an intention to embody gratitude that day. Tuesday might be attentiveness. Wednesday might be curiosity, and so on.

- **Give yourself a temporary tattoo.** Make it represent a value or committed action you want to work on. For example, you might write "courage" on the inside of your wrist if you want to practice brave actions, or you might draw a heart on your ankle if you want to embrace love and commit to giving affection. Maybe you like "moMEnt" to remind you to choose the Me you want to be in each present moment.

- **Choose a charm.** Select a small object to represent an internal experience that commonly shows up as an obstacle to committed action. For example, you might choose a Bashful Dwarf keychain to represent social anxiety, or a paperweight to represent heaviness or apathy. Place it in your pocket or on your shoulder and walk around with it; buckle it into a seat belt or car seat and drive around with it; put it under your pillow or on the pillow next to you and sleep with it. Experience moving your hands, feet, and mouth in values-consistent ways while bringing the would-be barrier object along with you.

- **Consider your epitaph.** When you come to a crossroads that requires a choice between a comfortable, familiar path versus an uncertain, less comfortable choice, consider how this would be reflected in your epitaph: "Here lies Jane, sedentary cookie eater" versus "Here lies Jane, active adventurous role model mama." Ask yourself, *What do I want to stand for?*

- **Create a personal motto.** Based on the Me you want to be, allow your personal motto to guide your choices for the day. For example, if your motto is "Work hard, play hard" you might spend part of your day kicking butt at the office and the other part at happy hour with friends.

MINDFULNESS, DEFUSION, AND SELF

One may walk over the highest mountain, one step at a time.

—Barbara Walters

We develop psychological flexibility by (1) cultivating mindfulness—purposeful, nonjudgmental, flexible attention to what is present inside and outside our skin in this one moment—which creates a space (2) for acceptance of emotions and sensations, and (3) defusion—impassive observation of thoughts and self-stories from the (4) perspective of a self who has thoughts but is separate from them (we are not our thoughts), which (5) replaces our reactive-autopilot default with greater freedom to make conscious, deliberate, values-driven choices.

We may be particularly vulnerable to psychological *inflexibility* when core beliefs, schemas, or self-stories—developed during childhood or adolescence as a way to make sense of our early experiences—get triggered. This is because these old thoughts tend to partner with well-worn behaviors that developed to provide protection during youth but are rarely values congruent as adults. Still, we can mindfully watch out for our schemas and their associated urges, then defuse (by stepping back and observing thoughts or robbing their authority with silliness), accept, and choose valued actions.

ACT processes can empower you to live a full life—even after a long history of abuse and depression, such as with Ingrid.

Ingrid's Story

My first bout of debilitating depression occurred in my first year at university at seventeen years old. Academically I was fine, but a new country and a completely different environment were very stressful. I felt overwhelmed by stress for the first time, which was very surprising, as I had come from a very abusive background.

Over the next thirty-five years or so, a pattern developed whereby stressful events, like moving, would mean a roughly two-year period before I emerged from my shell. I stayed very driven and seldom strayed from professional obligations or meetings. But I was often in self-survival mode by keeping up appearances, yet I was frozen inside.

ACT helped me a great deal at first to accept myself as a normal human being without shameful deficiencies. Mindfulness exercises were extremely beneficial from the start as I found peace in that "alone" place where I did not have the stress of other human beings. Through acceptance, I began to notice how terrified I felt at times, along with the people and contexts that triggered or exacerbated my fears. Through committed action I started a step-by-step approach to defend my boundaries. At times, I made mistakes, like being aggressive instead of assertive, which brought on the old story of shame, which helped me to clarify my values and what type of a person I want to be.

I cannot help but be amazed at who I am today. I recognize bullying behavior from others toward me much more quickly than I used to, and although I am still aware of fear inside me, I am more able to stand up for myself. Even having learned to choose my battles is a strength that I am now aware of: I don't often find myself wasting energy on an unimportant struggle with someone who will have no significant impact on my life.

Through training myself to "notice" internal events, I have more information about what brings me joy, like roses and music and certain scents. I now actively pursue a life that has such pleasures in it, as opposed to spending all my time just trying to stay out of harm's way. I am aware of my body and treat it more kindly through massage, scents, herbs, and so on. I am now living a fuller life and have not had a depressive episode for twelve years.

Ongoing Mindfulness and Defusion Practices

To continue your practice with mindfulness, defusion, self-as-context, and self-compassion, try some of the following:

- **Blow bubbles mindfully.** Breathe in fully, blow out slowly, watching the bubbles. Imagine one is a thought, and stand back observing it float and pop.

- **Blow (or imagine blowing) a dandelion.** Make sure it's the mature, white, fluffy kind. Breathe in fully, blow out slowly, and watch the seeds float about, allowing each one to represent an internal experience. Stand back and observe.

- **Play the balloon game.** Get one regular, inflated latex (not helium) balloon. Bobble the balloon from hand to hand, playing the "don't let the balloon hit the floor" game. Try to worry about the future, bringing to mind some of your typical what-if thoughts, all the while continuing to bobble the balloon, keeping it off the floor. Try to ruminate about the past, bringing to mind a regret or concern about a recent performance, all the while continuing to bobble the balloon, keeping it off the floor. Notice how you can't be in two "times" (for instance, present and future) at once. Active engagement with the balloon game brings your awareness back to the present when it drifts to the past or future. Importantly, the intention is not to avoid difficult thoughts but to experience the shift between past, present, and future, and to practice redirecting attention to the present when it travels forward or backward in time.

- **Get sensory.** Every so often, check in on one of your senses—notice what you smell; then notice who's noticing. Repeat with sight, hearing, and so on. Even now, see what you are reading. Then notice who is seeing it.

- **Dial in to your moments.** Show up and participate in your sweet moments as they arise. Notice and soak in what you see, hear, smell, taste, and feel. Do the same with moments that make you feel more alive. Notice the zhuzh. When you feel strong or empowered, pay attention to what you are doing, how you are doing it, where you are, and who you are with.

- **Take a self-compassion break** (Neff 2018). During times you are suffering, say something like, "This hurts, I'm not alone, may I be patient, may I hang in, may I be strong." You might also try cupping your face in your hands, much like you might a child who is dear to you, or placing a hand on your heart (skin to skin is most soothing) for added warmth and care. For a visual reminder, consider wearing a reversible "self-compassion it" wristband from this mighty compassion-focused nonprofit organization: https://compassionit.com/product/self-compassion -wristband/.

FINALLY LIVING FIERCE

Life is not measured by the number of breaths you take but by the moments that take your breath away.

—Maya Angelou

You know how anxiety is a big fan of questions? Most common, that what-if one? Well, I'd like to give you (and your anxiety, because we have space for her now too) some other questions to ask that might just help you live fiercely and flexibly by awakening your newly acquired ACT wisdom.

In this one moment, who is the Me I truly want to be?

If I listen to my mind (thoughts, self-stories, Inner Critic, memories, and so on) will it help me be the Me I want to be? Will it move me closer to the life I long for?

If I stay here, rooted in my Comfort Zone, what moments-that-matter might I miss?

If I let my unwanted feelings decide, what will it get me? What will it cost me?

And here's one more for good measure that includes every fundamental ACT process for building psychological flexibility:

With the wisdom that you are not your internal experiences (self-as-context), are you willing to step back from your thoughts (defusion) and fully allow your feelings, without resistance (acceptance), as they are, without judgment, in this one moment (mindfulness), and do what you care about (commitment) in ways that represent the Me you want to be (values)?

Now let's hear from Vanessa and her story of living fiercely and flexibly using her own question about choice.

Vanessa's Story

I have learned how to practice ACT most effectively through being around my children. My three-year-old has been my greatest teacher to date. Like many toddlers, she is a sponge and notices everything. She notices when the Mickey Mouse–shaped pancake has different-size ears, when the colors made from the new markers are brighter than the ones that have dried out, when the soil in the planter box is dry, when I buy a new kind of yogurt… She also notices when I am not giving her my attention.

There are some days I feel like Superwoman, balancing being a mom of two young children and working, cooking, cleaning, hosting, and more. Some days I think I need to do everything to be that Superwoman, like return work calls after-hours and respond to emails immediately, because somehow that will make me a more successful professional. My mind tells me I should work harder. I tell myself I am doing this because I am providing for my family. And while this may be true, it comes at a cost.

Toddler:	"Mommy, look!" [holding up her artwork at my feet]
Me:	[typing on my phone]
Toddler:	"Mommy!"
Me:	"Give me one second, I am almost done with this."
Toddler:	[walks away back to her art table]

Ouch. I am often very attentive to my kids, but I missed this moment. It hurt my daughter, and that hurt me. Even though there are several "look at me" moments with my kids, I missed this one. The "I'm not a good enough mom" story begins to play in my mind.

These missed moments happen far too often because my life is "so busy" that I feel like I am always trying to catch up on something. The truth is, I will always have work to do, but I won't always have my kids there wanting to show me their artwork.

This hurt did tell me something valuable about my love for my kids. The pain made me want to change.

When the phone rings, my eleven-month-old actually says, "Uh-oh" because she knows that the phone means attention away from her. So I now put my phone away when I am playing with my kids because I want to truly be present. I put my phone on silent so I don't become distracted by the sound of an incoming text or call. Sometimes I even put my phone in a different room so I'm less tempted to check it. The phone hiatus gets tricky when I try to capture a few pictures of my kiddos being adorable because, yet again, I am behind a screen. I am missing another moment when I am busy scrolling through the pictures to see if I got a good one.

So when I think about the missed moments, I know I have a choice, and I ask myself a question: Do I want to give in to the urges served up by my phone, or do I want to pick up a marker and join the coloring party?

ACT has helped me grow personally and professionally because it has made me constantly reevaluate what is important in my life and then reminds me that I have the choice to take steps away from suffering and toward living a more meaningful life. So when I stop and smell those pancakes, color outside the lines, get my hands dirty, look into my children's eyes and hear them laugh, I feel like I am not only witnessing the moment, I am part of it.

And Then There Was One

If you are extra perceptive, you may have noticed I said *five* fierce women were going to share their personal ACT stories, but I included only four. That's because I'm the fifth. I will keep it brief because I've already sprinkled a lot of my own experiences throughout the book.

While I am most definitely still an imperfect work in progress, I credit the past eighteen years of learning, living, and sharing ACT for giving me the tools to embrace pain and live, love, and labor out loud. Because of ACT, I experience sweetness when I show up to the small moments with my kids, my husband, my friends, and my dogs. I experience awe and wonder when I stop to fully notice the ocean view and breathtaking sunsets right outside my office. Because of ACT, I have made brave and daring choices in the face of fear and uncertainty that have granted me a rich and fulfilling career and an as-close-to-perfect work-life balance as I can imagine. Because of ACT, I feel deeply connected to my therapy clients.

Life hasn't gotten any less painful. On the contrary. The past five years have been unimaginably difficult in ways I would need an entire memoir to adequately describe. But because of ACT, I have not only survived the category 6 hurricane (metaphorically speaking) but have become more mighty in spite of it. Because of ACT, I like myself. Warts and all.

I AM WOMAN HEAR ME RULE

Before I leave you with the final takeaway, I want to come full circle from some of what you read in the very beginning of this book. I shared some research about the myriad ways women are marginalized (e.g., unequal pay, the pink tax, etc.), and posited that this may be partially related to the higher prevalence of anxiety, worry, and stress in women.

But there is a flip side to this. Are we battling gender disparity at nearly every turn? Yes. *And* research *also* shows:

- Patients treated by female physicians have lower mortality and hospital readmission rates than those treated by male physicians (Tsugawa et al. 2017).

- Women are less likely to die from a heart attack when treated by a female physician (Tsugawa et al. 2017).

- When women are represented on leadership teams, corporate financial performance dramatically improves (Hunt, Layton, and Prince 2015).

- When more women are involved in group decisions about land management, environmental conservation improves (Cook, Grillos, and Anderson 2019).

- Women are more likely than men to bring new and unique skills to professional boards, and these boards are more effective because of it (Daehyun and Starks 2016).

- When women participate in conflict prevention and resolution, peace agreements are less likely to fail (Paffenholz, Kew, and Wanis-St. John 2006) and more likely to endure (O'Reilly, Súilleabháin, and Paffenholz 2015).

- The lives of women and mothers improve when women enter the political arena: female legislators sponsor more bills and pass more laws that impact women's health and well-being, and they send their districts more money (Swers 2005; Anzia and Berry 2011).

This list also goes on and on. Women are fierce. We are powerful. We have so much to contribute to the personal and professional arena. My wish for you is that you continue your own ACT journey and emerge mightier with each psychologically flexible stride you take, whatever shape that may take. (And you can visit the Resources section in this book for additional ACT reading materials.)

THE FINAL TAKEAWAY

If there's one thing you've learned through your reading, it's that I have an apparent obsession with acronyms. It's a bit of a joke in the mental health community, actually, that we psychologists love our acronyms. I don't expect you will remember them all, but hopefully they've brought some eye-rolling-in-a-mom-joke-kind-of-way amusement. So for your final SMH moment, I give you **BE MIGHTY** (come on, what else would it be?):

Breathe

Explore present experience

Make space for feelings

Impartially observe thoughts

Give self-compassion

Highlight values

Take action

Yell from the rooftops!

Just kidding, I have one more, but this is really the last one, the true takeaway (and much easier to remember!). Being mighty means choosing a new way—a psychologically flexible way—to **LIVE**:

Listen for pain

Invite it in

Value

Expand your life

Acknowledgments

First and foremost, I would like to extend an enormous amount of gratitude and appreciation to the entire team at New Harbinger: Catharine Meyers for her guidance and enduring enthusiasm from the very first seed of an idea through several iterations (and years) of idea sculpting, until we finally landed right where we were meant to be all along; Jennifer Holder for her absolute brilliance as an editor who can magically make a book better a million ways and back without ever losing its original voice or spirit; Georgia Kolias for her responsiveness and keeping things organized; Marisa Solis for her impeccable copy editing; and the artists, marketing crew, and other behind-the-scenes folks for bringing *Be Mighty* to life.

I would also like to thank Bridget Asplund for being my right-hand woman, my second set of eyes, my researcher, my references fixer, and my unerring cheerleader. Her willingness to step in at any moment and enthusiastically help in any way I needed is endlessly appreciated and will never be forgotten.

I am eternally grateful to my many ACT and anxiety mentors, without whom this book and my beloved career would not exist. Among them are Sue Orsillo, Liz Roemer, Niloo Afari, Julie Wetherell, David Barlow, and Stefan Hofmann. Their knowledge, talent, generosity, and support are forever appreciated.

Ingrid Ord, Sarah Mooy, Shoshana Shea, Vanessa Laughter, and Bridget Asplund deserve special appreciation for their contributions of personal ACT stories. I'm moved by their journeys and their willingness to share their voices as women who wish to raise up other women.

To the ACBS community, and Women's SIG especially, I am grateful for the openness, generosity, and commitment to ongoing growth and development that I have continuously encountered there before, during, and sure to be after the writing of this book.

And to my clients whose willingness and courage inspire me to be mighty every single day. I learn as much from them as they do from me, and I am honored that they allow me to be a part of their journey.

Finally, my husband and children have my deepest gratitude for their patience and understanding while I was feverishly working away in the days leading up to my deadlines. Their loving support means the world to me. My husband is owed an extra thank-you for his humor, his willingness to humor me, and his clever contribution to the super-villain in chapter 9. I love you, my sweet family.

Resources

ACT Self-Help Books for Adult Anxiety

Forsyth, J., and G. Eifert. 2018. *Anxiety Happens: 52 Ways to Find Peace of Mind.* Oakland, CA: New Harbinger Publications.

Wilson, K., and T. Dufrene. 2010. *Things Might Go Terribly, Horribly Wrong: A Guide to Life Liberated from Anxiety.* Oakland, CA: New Harbinger Publications.

ACT Workbooks for Adult Anxiety and Stress

Fleming, J., and N. Kocovski. 2013. *The Mindfulness and Acceptance Workbook for Social Anxiety and Shyness: Using Acceptance and Commitment Therapy to Free Yourself from Fear and Reclaim Your Life.* Oakland, CA: New Harbinger Publications.

Folette, V., and J. Pistorello. 2007. *Finding Life Beyond Trauma: Using Acceptance and Commitment Therapy to Heal from Post-Traumatic Stress and Trauma-Related Problems.* Oakland, CA: New Harbinger Publications.

Forsyth, J., and G. Eifert. 2016. *The Mindfulness and Acceptance Workbook for Anxiety: A Guide to Breaking Free from Anxiety, Phobias, and Worry Using Acceptance and Commitment Therapy.* Oakland, CA: New Harbinger Publications.

Livhem, F., and F. Bond. 2018. *The Mindfulness and Acceptance Workbook for Stress Reduction: Using Acceptance and Commitment Therapy to Manage Stress, Build Resilience, and Create the Life You Want.* Oakland, CA: New Harbinger Publications.

ACT Books and Workbooks for Teens and Young Adults

Ciarrochi, J., and Hayes, L. 2012. *Get Out of Your Mind and into Your Life for Teens: A Guide to Living an Extraordinary Life*. Oakland, CA: New Harbinger Publications.

Fielding, L. 2019. *Mastering Adulthood: Go Beyond Adulting to Become an Emotional Grown-Up*. Oakland, CA: New Harbinger Publications.

Scarlet, J. 2017. *Superhero Therapy: Mindfulness Skills to Help Teens and Young Adults Deal with Anxiety, Depression, and Trauma*. Oakland, CA: New Harbinger Publications.

Sedley, B. 2017. *Stuff That Sucks: A Teen's Guide to Accepting What You Can't Change and Committing to What You Can*. Oakland, CA: New Harbinger Publications.

Turrell, S., and C. McCurry. 2018. *The Mindfulness and Acceptance Workbook for Teen Anxiety: Activities to Help You Overcome Fears and Worries Using Acceptance and Commitment Therapy*. Oakland, CA: New Harbinger Publications.

ACT Books for Parents

Coyne, L., and A. Murrell. 2009. *The Joy of Parenting: An Acceptance and Commitment Therapy Guide to Effective Parenting in the Early Years*. Oakland, CA: New Harbinger Publications.

McCurry, C. 2009. *Parenting Your Anxious Child with Mindfulness and Acceptance: A Powerful New Approach to Overcoming Fear, Panic, and Worry Using Acceptance and Commitment Therapy*. Oakland, CA: New Harbinger Publications.

Zurita Ona, P. 2017. *Parenting a Troubled Teen: Manage Conflict and Deal with Intense Emotions Using Acceptance and Commitment Therapy*. Oakland, CA: New Harbinger Publications.

References

American Psychiatric Association. 2013. *Diagnostic and Statistical Manual of Mental Disorders.* 5th ed. Arlington, VA: American Psychiatric Publishing.

Anzia, S. F., and C. R. Berry. 2011. "The Jackie (and Jill) Robinson Effect: Why Do Congresswomen Outperform Congressmen?" *American Journal of Political Science* 55: 478–493.

Arch, J. J., G. H. Eifert, C. Davies, J. Vilardaga, R. D. Rose, and M. G. Craske. 2012. "Randomized Clinical Trial of Cognitive Behavioral Therapy (CBT) versus Acceptance and Commitment Therapy (ACT) for Mixed Anxiety Disorders." *Journal of Consulting and Clinical Psychology* 80: 750–765.

Babcock, L., M. P. Recalde, L. Vesterlund, and L. Weingart. 2017. "Gender Differences in Accepting and Receiving Requests for Tasks with Low Promotability." *American Economic Review* 107: 714–747.

Barlow, D. H. 2002. *Anxiety and Its Disorders,* 2nd ed. New York: Guilford Press.

Baumeister, R. F., J. D. Campbell, J. L., Krueger, and K. D. Vohs. 2003. "Does High Self-Esteem Cause Better Performance, Interpersonal Success, Happiness, or Healthier Lifestyles?" *Psychological Science in the Public Interest* 4: 1–44.

Beck, A. T. 1967. *Depression: Clinical, Experimental, and Theoretical Aspects.* New York: Harper Row.

Bishu, S. G., and M. G. Alkadry. 2017. "A Systematic Review of the Gender Pay Gap and Factors That Predict It." *Administration & Society* 49: 65–104.

Black, M. C., K. C. Basile, M. J. Breiding, S. G. Smith, M. L. Walters, M. T. Merrick, J. Chen, and M. R. Stevens. 2011. *The National Intimate Partner and Sexual Violence Survey (NISVS): 2010 Summary Report.* Atlanta, GA: National Center for Injury Prevention and Control, Centers for Disease Control and Prevention.

Bouton, M. 2014. "Why Behavior Change Is Difficult to Sustain." *Preventive Medicine* 68: 29–36.

Brescoll, V. L., and E. L. Uhlmann. 2008. "Can an Angry Woman Get Ahead? Status Conferral, Gender, and Expression of Emotion in the Workplace." *Psychological Science* 19: 268–275.

Brescoll, V. L., E. Dawson, and E. L. Uhlmann. 2010. "Hard Won and Easily Lost: The Fragile Status of Leaders in Gender-Stereotype-Incongruent Occupations." *Psychological Science* 21: 1640–1642.

Bromberg-Martin, E. S., and O. Hikosaka. 2009. "Midbrain Dopamine Neurons Signal Preference for Advance Information About Upcoming Rewards." *Neuron* 63: 119–126.

Butler, K. 2014. *Text quotes.* Retrieved from https://lessonslearned inlife.com/text-quotes/

Campbell-Sills, L., D. H. Barlow, T. A. Brown, and S. G. Hofmann. 2006. "Effects of Suppression and Acceptance on Emotional Responses of Individuals with Anxiety and Mood Disorders." *Behaviour Research and Therapy* 44: 1251–1263. https://doi.org/10 .1016/j.brat.2005.10.001

Cannon, W. B. 1929. *Bodily Changes in Pain, Hunger, Fear, and Rage: Researches into the Function of Emotional Excitement.* New York: Harper and Row.

Carleton, R. N. 2016. "Into the Unknown: A Review and Synthesis of Contemporary Models Involving Uncertainty." *Journal of Anxiety Disorders* 39: 30–43.

Carvalho, S., A. Dinis, J. Pinto-Gouveia, and C. Estanqueiro. 2015. "Memories of Shame Experiences with Others and Depression Symptoms: The Mediating Role of Experiential Avoidance." *Clinical Psychology and Psychotherapy* 22: 32–44.

Cook, N. J., T. Grillos, and K. P. Anderson. 2019. "Gender Quotas increase the Equality and Effectiveness of Climate Policy Interventions." *Nature Climate Change* 9: 330–334.

Daehyun, K., and L. T. Starks. 2016. "Gender Diversity on Corporate Boards: Do Women Contribute Unique Skills?" *American Economic Review* 106: 267–71.

De Berker, A. O., R. B. Rutledge, C. Mathys, L. Marshall, G. F. Cross, R. J. Dolan, and S. Bestmann. 2016. "Computations of Uncertainty Mediate Acute Stress Responses in Humans." *Nature Communications* 7: 1–11.

De Blasio, B., and J. Menin. 2015. "From Cradle to Cane: The Cost of Being a Female Consumer. A study of Gender Pricing in New York City." *The New York Department of Consumer Affairs.* Accessed November 10, 2018. https://www1.nyc.gov/assets/dca /downloads/pdf/partners/Study-of-Gender-Pricing-in-NYC.pdf

D'Zurilla, T. J., and A. M. Nezu. 2006. *Problem-Solving Therapy: A Positive Approach to Clinical Intervention.* 3rd ed. New York: Springer.

Eilenberg, T., P. Fink, J. S. Jensen, W. Rief, and L. Frostholm. 2016. "Acceptance and Commitment Group Therapy (ACT-G) for Health Anxiety: A Randomized Controlled Trial." *Psychological Medicine* 46: 103–115.

Files, J. A., A. P. Mayer, M. G. Ko, P. Friedrich, M. Jenkins, M. J. Bryan, S. Vegunta, C. M. Wittich, M. A. Lyle, R. Melikian, T. Duston, Y. H. Chang, and S. N. Hayes. 2017. "Speaker Introductions at Internal Medicine Grand Rounds: Forms of Address Reveal Gender Bias." *Journal of Women's Health* 26: 413–419.

Finkelhor, D., G. Hotaling, I. A. Lewis, and C. Smith. 1990. "Sexual Abuse in a National Survey of Adult Men and Women: Prevalence, Characteristics, and Risk Factors." *Child Abuse & Neglect* 14: 19–28.

Forman, E. M., J. D. Herbert, E. Moitra, P. D. Yeomans, and P. A. Geller. 2007. "A Randomized Controlled Effectiveness Trial of Acceptance and Commitment Therapy and Cognitive Therapy for Anxiety and Depression." *Behavior Modification* 31: 772–799.

Forsyth, J. P., and G. H. Eifert. 1996. "The Language of Feeling and the Feeling of Anxiety: Contributions of the Behaviorisms Toward Understanding the Function-Altering Effects of Language." *The Psychological Record* 46: 607–649.

Grabe, S., L. M. Ward, and J. S. Hyde. 2008. "The Role of the Media in Body Image Concerns Among Women: A Meta-Analysis of Experimental and Correlational Studies." *Psychological Bulletin* 134: 460–476.

Hayes, S., D. Barnes-Holmes, and B. Roche, eds. 2001. *Relational Frame Theory: A Post-Skinnerian Account of Human Language and Cognition.* New York: Plenum Press.

Hayes, L. L., and J. Ciarrochi. 2015. *The Thriving Adolescent: Using Acceptance and Commitment Therapy and Positive Psychology to Help Teens Manage Emotions, Achieve Goals, and Build Connection.* Oakland, CA: New Harbinger Publications.

Hayes, S., and S. Smith. 2005. *Get Out of Your Mind and Into Your Life: The New Acceptance and Commitment Therapy.* Oakland, CA: New Harbinger Publications.

Hayes, S., K. Strosahl, and K. Wilson. 1999. *Acceptance and Commitment Therapy: An Experiential Approach to Behavior Change.* New York: Guilford Press.

Hayes, S., K. Strosahl, and K. Wilson. 2012. *Acceptance and Commitment Therapy: The Process and Practice of Mindful Change.* New York: Guilford Press.

Heilman, M. E., A. S. Wallen, D. Fuchs, and M. M. Tamkins. 2004. "Penalties for Success: Reactions to Women Who Succeed at Male Gender-Typed Tasks." *Journal of Applied Psychology* 89: 416–427.

Hooper, N., K. E. Sandoz, J. Ashton, A. Clarke, and L. McHugh. 2012. "Comparing Thought Suppression and Acceptance as Coping Techniques for Food Cravings." *Eating Behaviors* 13: 62–64.

Hunt, V., D. Layton, and S. Prince. 2015. "Why Diversity Matters." *McKinsey and Company Annual Report.* Accessed March 24, 2019. https://www.mckinsey.com/business-functions/organization/our-insights/why-diversity-matters.

Joshi, A., J. Son, and H. Roh. 2015. "When Can Women Close I gap? A Meta-Analytic Test of Sex Differences in Performance and Rewards." *Academy of Management Journal* 58: 1516–1545.

Kabat-Zinn, J. 1994. *Wherever You Go There You Are: Mindfulness Meditation in Everyday Life.* New York: Hyperion.

Kannan, D., and H. M. Levitt. 2013. "A Review of Client Self-Criticism in Psychotherapy." *Journal of Psychotherapy Integration* 23: 166–178.

Karpowitz, C. F., T. Mendelberg, and L. Shaker. 2012. "Gender Inequality in Deliberative Participation." *American Political Science Review* 106: 533–547.

Kessler, R. C., W. Tat Chiu, O. Demler, and E. E. Walters. 2005. "Prevalence, Severity, and Comorbidity of 12-Month DSM-IV Disorders in the National Comorbidity Survey Replication." *Archives of General Psychiatry* 62: 617–627.

Kolts, R. L. 2016. *CFT Made Simple.* Oakland, CA: New Harbinger Publications.

Lamott, A. 2017. "12 Truths I Learned from Life and Writing." Filmed April 2017 in Vancouver, BC. From Ted video https://www.ted.com/talks/anne_lamott_12_truths_i_learned_from_life_and_writing

Lazarus, R. S. 1991. "Progress on a Cognitive-Motivational-Relational Theory of Emotion." *American Psychologist* 46: 819–834.

Levitt, J. T., T. A. Brown, S. M. Orsillo, and D. H. Barlow. 2004. "The Effects of Acceptance Versus Suppression of Emotion on Subjective and Psychophysiological Response to Carbon Dioxide Challenge in Patients with Panic Disorder." *Behavior Therapy* 35: 747–766.

Liddell, H. S. 1949. "The Role of Vigilance in the Development of Animal Neurosis." In P. Hoch and I. Zubin (Eds.) *Anxiety*. New York: Grune & Stratton.

Liverant, G. I., T. A. Brown, D. H. Barlow, and L. Roemer. 2008. "Emotion Regulation in Unipolar Depression: The Effects of Acceptance and Suppression of Subjective Emotional Experience on the Intensity and Duration of Sadness annd Negative Affect." *Behaviour Research and Therapy* 46: 1201–1209.

Luoma, J. B., S. C. Hayes, and R. C. Walser. 2007. *Learning ACT: An Acceptance & Commitment Therapy Skills-Training Manual for Therapists*. Oakland, CA: New Harbinger, and Reno, NV: Context Press.

Marks, I. M., and R. M. Nesse. 1994. "Fear and Fitness: An Evolutionary Analysis of Anxiety Disorders." *Ethology and Sociobiology* 15: 247–261.

Masedo, A. I., and M. R. Esteve. 2007. "Effects of Suppression, Acceptance, and Spontaneous Coping on Pain Tolerance, Pain Intensity, and Distress." *Behaviour Research and Therapy* 45: 199–209.

McGonigal, K. 2013. "How to Make Stress Your Friend." Filmed June 2013 in Edinburgh, Scotland. TED video, 13:21. https://www.ted .com/talks/elly_mcgonigal_how_to_make_stress_your_friend /transcript

McKay, M., A. Lev, and M. Skeen. 2012. *Acceptance and Commitment Therapy for Interpersonal Problems: Using Mindfulness, Acceptance, and Schema Awareness to Change Interpersonal Behaviors*. Oakland, CA: New Harbinger Publications.

Nakamura, J., and M. Csikszentmihalyi. 2009. "Flow Theory and Research." In C. R. Snyder and S. J. Lopez (Eds.) *The Oxford Handbook of Positive Psychology*. 2nd ed. New York: Oxford University Press, Inc.

Neff, K. D. 2003. "Self-Compassion: An Alternative Conceptualization of a Healthy Attitude Toward Oneself." *Self and Identity* 2: 85–102.

Neff, K. D. 2008. "Self-Compassion: Moving Beyond the Pitfalls of a Separate Self-Concept." In J. Bauer and H. A. Wayment (Eds.) *Transcending Self-Interest: Psychological Explorations of the Quiet Ego*. Washington, DC: APA Books.

Neff, K. D. 2011. "Self-Compassion, Self-Esteem, and Well-Being." *Social and Personality Psychology Compass* 5: 1–12.

Neff, K. D. 2018. "Exercise 2: Self-Compassion Break." Accessed November 10, 2018. https://self-compassion.org/exercise-2-self-compassion-break/.

Neff, K. D., K. Kirkpatrick, and S. S. Rude. 2007. "Self-Compassion and Its Link to Adaptive Psychological Functioning." *Journal of Research in Personality* 41: 139–154.

Neff, K. D., S. S. Rude, and K. Kirkpatrick. 2007. "An Examination of Self-Compassion in Relation to Positive Psychological Functioning and Personality Traits." *Journal of Research in Personality* 41: 908–916.

Neff, K., and R. Vonk. 2009. "Self-Compassion versus Global Self-Esteem: Two Different Ways of Relating to Oneself." *Journal of Personality* 77: 23–50.

Nesse, R. M. 1987. "An Evolutionary Perspective on Panic Disorder and Agoraphobia." *Ethology and Sociobiology* 8: 73S–83S.

Nesse, R. M. 1998. "Emotional Disorders in Evolutionary Perspective." *British Journal of Medical Psychology* 71: 397–415.

Nesse, R. M. 2001. "The Smoke Detector Principle: Natural Selection and the Regulation of Defenses." *Annals of the New York Academy of Sciences* 935: 75–85.

O'Reilly, M., A. Ó Súilleabháin, and T. Paffenholz. 2015. "Reimagining Peacemaking: Women's Roles in Peace Processes," New York: International Peace Institute.

Orsillo, S. M., and Roemer, L. 2011. *The Mindful Way Through Anxiety: Break Free From Chronic Worry and Reclaim Your Life*. New York, NY: Guilford Press.

Paffenholz, T., D. Kew, and A. Wanis-St. John. 2006. *Civil Society and Peace Negotiations: Why, Whether and How They Could be Involved.* Paper presented at the International Studies Association Conference, March, San Diego, CA.

Park, L. E., A. F. Young, and P. W. Eastwick. 2015. "Psychological Distance Makes the Heart Grow Fonder: Effects of Psychological Distance and Relative Intelligence on Men's Attraction to Women." *Personality and Social Psychology Bulletin* 4: 1459–1473.

Pew Research Center. 2015. "Raising Kids and Running a Household: How Working Parents Share the Load." Accessed November 10, 2018. http://www.pewsocialtrends.org/2015/11/04/raising-kids-and -running-a-household-how-working-parents-share-the-load/

Raes, F. 2010. "Rumination and Worry as Mediators of the Relation-ship Between Self-Compassion and Depression and Anxiety." *Personality & Individual Differences* 48: 757–761.

Ritzert, T. R., J. P. Forsyth, S. C. Sheppard, J. F. Boswell, C. R. Berghoff, and G. H. Eifert. 2016. "Evaluating the Effectiveness of ACT for Anxiety Disorders in a Self-Help Context: Outcomes from a Randomized Wait-List Controlled Trial." *Behavior Therapy* 47 (4): 444–459.

Roediger, E., B. A. Stevens, and R. Brockman. 2018. *Contextual Schema Therapy: An Integrative Approach to Personality Disorders, Emotional Dysregulation, & Interpersonal Functioning.* Oakland, CA: New Harbinger Publications.

Roelofs, K. 2017. "Freeze for Action: Neurobiological Mechanisms in Animal and Human Freezing." *Philosophical Transactions of the Royal Society B: Biological Sciences* 372: 1,718.

Roemer, L., S. M. Orsillo, and K. Salters-Pedneault. 2008. "Efficacy of an Acceptance-Based Behavior Therapy for Generalized Anxiety Disorder: Evaluation in a Randomized Controlled Trial." *Journal of Consulting and Clinical Psychology* 76: 1083–1089.

Rudman, L. A., and P. Glick. 1999. "Feminized Management and Backlash Toward Agentic Women: The Hidden Costs to Women of a Kinder, Gentler Image of Middle Managers." *Journal of Personality and Social Psychology* 77: 1004–1010.

Scarlet, J. 2018. "Defining Your Origin Story." Superhero Therapy. Accessed August 15, 2018. http://www.superhero-therapy.com /defining-your-origin-story/

Stoddard, J. A., and N. Afari. 2014. *The Big Book of ACT Metaphors: A Practitioner's Guide to Experiential Exercises and Metaphors in Acceptance and Commitment Therapy.* Oakland, CA: New Harbinger Publications.

Stowe, H. B. 1856. *Dred: A Tale of the Great Dismal Swamp.* London: Phillips, Sampson and Company.

Swers, M. L. 2005. "Connecting Descriptive and Substantive Representation: An Analysis of Sex Differences in Cosponsorship Activity." *Legislative Studies Quarterly* 30 (3): 407–433.

Tirch, D., B. Schoendorff, and L. R. Silberstein. 2014. *The ACT Practitioner's Guide to the Science of Compassion: Tools for Fostering Psychological Flexibility.* Oakland, CA: New Harbinger Publications.

Tsugawa Y., A. B. Jena, J. F. Figueroa, E. J. Orav, D. M. Blumenthal, and A. K. Jha. 2017. "Comparison of Hospital Mortality and Readmission Rates for Medicare Patients Treated by Male vs Female Physicians." *JAMA Internal Medicine* 177: 206–213.

Waldinger, R. 2015. "What Makes a Good Life? Lessons from the Longest Study on Happiness." Filmed November 2015 in Brookline, MA. TED video, 12:48. https://www.ted.com/talks /robert_waldinger_what_makes_a_good_life_lessons_from_the _longest_study_on_happiness?language=en

Walser, R., and Westrup, D. 2007. *Acceptance & Commitment Therapy for the Treatment of Post-Traumatic Stress Disorder & Trauma-Related Problems: A Practitioner's Guide to Using Mindfulness & Acceptance Strategies.* Oakland, CA: New Harbinger.

Wegner, D. M. 1994. "Ironic Processes of Mental Control." *Psychological Review* 101: 34–52.

Wenzlaff, R. M., and D. M. Wegner. 2000. "Thought Suppression." *Annual Review of Psychology* 51: 59–91.

Wetherell, J. L., N. Afari, C. R. Ayers, J. A. Stoddard, J. Ruberg, J. T. Sorrell, et al. 2011. "Acceptance and Commitment Therapy for Generalized Anxiety Disorder in Older Adults: A Preliminary Report." *Behavior Therapy* 42: 127–134.

Whelton, W. J., and L. S. Greenberg. 2005. "Emotion in Self-Criticism." *Personality and Individual Differences* 38: 1583–1595.

Wilson, K. G. 2018. "Self-Care, Kindness, and Living Well with Dr. Kelly Wilson." *Psychologists Off the Clock*. Recorded November 13, 2018, by cohost Diana Hill. Audio podcast, 1:01:23. Retrieved from https://www.offtheclockpsych.com/podcast/science-of-kindness?rq=kelly%20wilson

Wilson, K. G., and T. DuFrene. 2009. *Mindfulness for Two: An Acceptance and Commitment Therapy Approach to Mindfulness in Psychotherapy*. Oakland, CA: New Harbinger.

Wood, J. V., W. Q. E. Perunovic, and J. W. Lee. 2009. "Positive Self-Statements: Power for Some, Peril for Others." *Psychological Science* 20: 860–866.

World Health Organization. 2017. *Depression and Other Common Mental Disorders: Global Health Estimates*. Geneva: World Health Organization.

Yerkes, R. M., and J. D. Dodson. 1908. "The Relation of Strength of Stimulus to Rapidity of Habit-Formation." *Journal of Comparative Neurology and Psychology* 18: 459–482.

Young, J. E., J. S. Klosko, and M. E. Weishaar. 2003. *Schema Therapy: A Practitioner's Guide*. New York: Guilford.

Jill A. Stoddard, PhD, is founder and director of The Center for Stress and Anxiety Management, a multisite outpatient clinic in San Diego, CA. She specializes in acceptance and commitment therapy (ACT) and cognitive behavioral therapy (CBT) for anxiety and related issues. Stoddard received her PhD in clinical psychology from Boston University in 2007. She is an award-winning teacher, recognized ACT trainer, and coauthor of *The Big Book of ACT Metaphors*. She lives in San Diego with her husband, two kids, and two French bulldogs.

MORE BOOKS *from*
NEW HARBINGER PUBLICATIONS

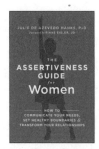

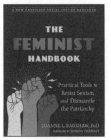

Register your **new harbinger** titles for additional benefits!

When you register your **new harbinger** title—purchased in any format, from any source—you get access to benefits like the following:

- Downloadable accessories like printable worksheets and extra content
- Instructional videos and audio files
- Information about updates, corrections, and new editions

Not every title has accessories, but we're adding new material all the time.

Access free accessories in 3 easy steps:

1. Sign in at NewHarbinger.com (or **register** to create an account).

2. Click on **register a book**. Search for your title and click the **register** button when it appears.

3. Click on the **book cover or title** to go to its details page. Click on **accessories** to view and access files.

That's all there is to it!

If you need help, visit:

NewHarbinger.com/accessories

new harbinger
CELEBRATING
40 YEARS